WHAT COUNTS MOST IS HOW YOU FINISH

WHAT COUNTS MOST IS HOW YOU FINISH

Thoughts on Living
Life to the Fullest

Jackie,
Happy birthday.
Keep doing what you're
doing and you'll finish
well. Shelia
Feb. 13, 2019

Shelia Payton

To order additional copies of this book, contact:
Xlibris Corporation
1-888-795-4274
www.Xlibris.com
Orders@Xlibris.com
38822

Dedication

This book is dedicated to my parents, grandparents and generations past whose example, wisdom and counsel helped guide my life; and to my nieces, nephew and future generations of young people who have within them the ability to shape a better world for themselves and others.

Contents

DEALING WITH PEOPLE

OVERCOMING CHALLENGES

STAYING FOCUSED

ACHIEVING SUCCESS

MAKING A DIFFERENCE

ACKNOWLEDGEMENTS

It was important to me to make sure these essays made sense to someone other than myself. Therefore, I asked for honest feedback from those who would likely read the book. I truly appreciate the young people who took time out of their lives to read sections of the book, and were willing to provide candid comments about what they read. Specifically, I would like to thank my niece, Joi Michelle Payton; Marquinn Allen, Jhanisha Borum, Javaris Bradford, Armani Hughes, Deysha Smith-Jenkins; and the 38 students at Milwaukee Public School's Wisconsin Conservatory of Life Long Learning.

I also want to thank the adults who played a role in bringing this book to life:

- Sallie Brown, former principal of the Wisconsin Conservatory of Life Long Learning, who arranged for me to have some of her students participate in a discussion about the book.
- Matthew Gagnier—advanced English teacher at the Wisconsin Conservatory of Life Long Learning—for incorporating the reading and discussion project into his curriculum, and ensuring that his students followed through on the project. His efforts made it possible to get invaluable feedback.
- Vanessa Key and Ava Hillard of New Concept Self Development Center, for helping to recruit students.

- Jackie Moore Bowles of Creative Marketing Resources and former Jack & Jill president, who connected me to Joyce Feaster.
- Joyce Feaster, Jack & Jill Milwaukee Chapter president, who helped with recruiting and connected me with Shanee Jenkins of the Northside YMCA of Metropolitan Milwaukee.
- Shanee Jenkins, Director of the Northside YMCA, who made the branch available as a meeting place and helped recruit participants.
- Rayven Gordon and Julie Borum of the YMCA, for their recruitment assistance and help making the meetings flow smoothly.
- Jomania Wriddley who, though older than the target reader, brought perspective to the work.
- Dee Butler, Director of the Daniels-Mardak Boys & Girls Club, who provided direction regarding titling the book and whether to do separate books for males and females.
- Lora Hyler of Hyler Communications for connecting me with editor Anne Bingham.
- Anne Bingham for editorial suggestions that improved the final manuscript.
- My mother, Gertrude Payton, for doing a final review of the manuscript.

BEING YOU

Being Different is Hard

Being different is hard. People may not feel comfortable around you if you don't fit their idea of who you should be. For example, if you're a person of color, people will often make assumptions about who you are, what your background is, how you should act, what your lifestyle is like. Even within your own race, people may question your "authenticity" if you don't behave, dress, talk, or act the way they think you should. If you're a male, the stereotype is that you must be unemotional, tough, aggressive, a sports fan, and act and look a certain way. If you're a female the stereotype is that you must dress a certain way, be emotional, always try to please someone else, and hide your intellect.

I have been "different" (I prefer to use the word non-traditional) all my life because of the way I grew up. One of the gifts my parents gave me was the gift of curiosity. They encouraged me to be open to learning and trying new things. I had doll babies and tea sets, but I also learned to dribble and shoot a basketball, hit a baseball, play tennis, and bait my own hook when my family went fishing. For Christmas, in addition to traditional girl toys, I got a chemistry set one year, and a red and blue plastic printing press another year (a foreshadowing of my career as a writer). I was taught to do my best academically and not hide my ability to think just because I'm a girl. When my junior high school music appreciation teacher—Ralph Ullenberg—sent a note home suggesting I take violin lessons and join the school orchestra, my parents encouraged me to do that. That was the beginning of my love for classical music.

Growing up female and Negro (the term that was used when I was a child in the 1950's) these "unusual" attitudes, interests and behaviors created problems for some of my classmates. In fifth and sixth grade, I became the target of Negro bullies who didn't like the fact that I was a bookworm and got good grades. One day at recess I was sitting on an outdoor basement window sill because the other kids wouldn't play with me. A group of kids piled on my lap, pushed back against me and almost smothered me. Later they started waiting for me after school everyday to beat me up. Were it not for Miss Henrietta K. Hardy, the school principal who let me stay in her office after school until the crowd disappeared, I might have been seriously hurt. Another time a girl I considered my best friend set me up to be beaten up by a boy in our grade school by telling him I had started a rumor that he was a juvenile delinquent. In fact, I had not *started* the rumor. I had repeated something someone told me. (This experience taught me never to repeat gossip.) My babysitter heard the fight outside the back door of my house, and came out to run the boy off. When my father found out what happened, he went over to the boy's house to get things straightened out. The boy's father punished him, and I never had any problems with the boy again. In seventh and eighth grade, I became the target of white bullies at my junior high school. They would trip me on the playground, jostle me in the halls and call me names because I was attending "their" school and had the nerve to act like I belonged there. I was one of only two black students in the entire school. I got the last word, however, when I graduated as one of the top students in the school. While walking across the stage to get my certificate, I heard loud cheers from the audience. When I glanced around to see what was going on, some of the same people who had been my tormentors were standing on their feet applauding me. I guess that was their way of letting me know that, since they hadn't broken my spirit, I had earned their respect.

In college during the sixties "revolution" a black dorm mate challenged my blackness because I didn't wear my hair in an Afro. (This was the same woman who, the year before the "revolution" began would walk past the black cleaning woman in our dorm without speaking.) Truth be told, I had been thinking about growing an Afro, but after her comment I decided to stay with the press and curl straight hair look. I knew I was black; I'd identified with my culture before the "revolution." My parents had taught me to be proud of who I am. I was also taught to treat all people with respect, and not "look down" on or "up to" anyone based on how much money they had or the type of work they did. Therefore, I not only spoke to the black cleaning lady, but adopted her as a surrogate mother—a friendly and familiar face during my first time away from home. My blackness was not based on something as superficial as how I wore my hair.

I used another gift my parents gave me when I made a decision about what career to pursue—the gift of believing I could do anything I set my mind to. I remember my father telling me, "Don't take a back seat to anyone." So even during the days of segregation and overt prejudice, I felt I was somebody—not better than someone else, but equal to them. Therefore, I believed, my career options were wide open. In my junior year in high school I decided to major in journalism and become a newspaper reporter. I made that decision because I love to write, and because I believed journalism was a way to make a difference in the world. I had seen the difference media coverage made in the struggle for civil rights, and I wanted to be part of that change process. In 1965, I couldn't name one woman or one African American who worked for major media. I'm sure there were some, but their numbers were so small that I wasn't aware of them. When I told people about my plans, just about everybody told me I'd never get a job because *they* wouldn't hire a Black person or a woman. The doubters told me I should become a teacher or social worker—professions open to my race and gender. I certainly respected those fields. My mother was a teacher and my father was a social worker. But I wanted to be a writer and make a difference in the world through my writing. Journalism was the field in which I felt I could do *both*. Fortunately for me, my parents supported my dream. Their only suggestion was that I have a back-up plan in case I couldn't get a job in that field right away.

I did my homework, looking through the *World Book Encyclopedia* to find a university that had a school of journalism rather than just a department. (Home computers didn't exist back then.) I figured a place with a school of journalism would have more to offer and, therefore, provide a better education. I also wanted a school that had 10,000 students or fewer because I didn't want to get lost in the crowd at a large university. Syracuse University met both criteria and (it turned out) was one of the top journalism programs in the country.

Even though I was going to one of the top schools in the country, many people remained skeptical that I would find employment. I didn't let their doubts change my career plans. My decision to stay the course I had set for myself worked out. Between my junior year in high school and the time I graduated from Syracuse, the job market turned 180 degrees. Major media were looking to hire African Americans for their staff. I received a journalism award from Syracuse. A story about this was sent to media around the country, which may have helped me get an internship at the *Rochester* (N.Y.) *Democrat and Chronicle* the summer between graduating from Syracuse and attending graduate school at the University of Wisconsin—Milwaukee. Ron Martin (my boss at the *Democrat and Chronicle*) offered me a job at the paper he was moving to—the *Miami Herald*. I told Ron I was going to graduate school. He asked when I would be done. I told him in August of the next year. He took my phone number, and called me the following July to offer me the job again. I also received offers from my hometown paper (the *Milwaukee Journal*) and United Press International (UPI)—a service that covered stories from around the world and sent them to media outlets worldwide. I accepted the job at the *Herald*, which (at the time) was one of the top 10 papers in the country. To go from college to work for one of the top newspapers, and to receive an offer from UPI was almost unheard of for anyone. Normally people had to start at smaller publications and work their way up. But times had changed, and people like me—educated and of color—were in demand.

At the *Herald* I was on duty covering President Richard Nixon's movements at the "Florida White House" when the Watergate scandal broke. I was the first from my newspaper to learn about the break-in. I relayed that information to my editor. The story was assigned to the paper's investigative reporters (Jim Savage and Michael Baxter), who played a role in uncovering the details that led to the President's resignation from office. As a reporter I also won a Florida Press Club award for a series my co-worker (Gayle Pollard) and I did on the impact the economic recession of the 1970's was having on people in the central city.

Had I listened to those who told me I would never be hired as a newspaper reporter instead of to my parents, those opportunities would never have come my way, and my life would have turned out very differently. My work at the *Herald* prepared me for my next career move: public relations at the Miller Brewing Company.

Over the years, being non-traditional continued to be part of my life. In my early 30s when I was working at Miller, a co-worker (trying to be helpful, I guess) told me if I wanted to get a promotion to manager I needed to wear shorter skirts. I didn't, and got the promotion anyway—although I did train two male co-workers who became my supervisors before I finally got the promotion. One of them didn't have a college degree. I had a master's degree. Instead of being bitter about that, I stepped my "A" game up to my "A+" game—making it harder for those in charge to deny me a promotion. When you're moving into non-traditional territory you often have to work twice as hard to get what you deserve. But it ultimately pays off. In my case, I got the promotion to manager. My photo and a short article about the promotion ran in *Ebony* magazine. But even if I had not received a promotion on that job, I still was a winner. As my parents taught me, whatever you learn goes with you. So the fact that I had to work twice as hard and know twice as much to get a promotion meant this extra knowledge was available to me when I started my own business. While serving as a manager at Miller, I handled public relations nationally for two brands, and also some general public relations for the company as a whole. I also developed and managed a six-figure budget. The business skills I acquired as a manager made it possible for me to start my own business and run a small business development program at the University of Wisconsin—Milwaukee. That program was so successful that after the three-year foundation grant ran out Lamonte Brown (who was familiar with the program) helped get funds to continue the course by including it in the University's budget. I ran the program for 17 years, which allowed me to earn a retirement pension, and semi-retire at age 55. Being semi-retired at an early age is giving me an opportunity to do some of the things I've always wanted to do—including writing. None of this would have happened had I listened to those naysayers in 1965 who said a Black woman could not get a job as a reporter with a major newspaper.

Going into a field where women or people of color traditionally have not worked before, or doing something else non-traditional is not easy. There will always be people who aren't happy about you doing what you're doing. Some of them will try to undermine your success. A few years ago I had an African American male refuse to advertise in the *Wisconsin Black Pages* business directory that I publish (even though he wanted to let African Americans know about the medical care gap between Blacks and the larger society). His problem: he saw where I sat at a Milwaukee Bucks basketball game and decided "I didn't need the money." Obviously, if he saw me at the game he was there too; so I don't understand why my being there was an issue. I doubt he would have said something like that if I had been a sales person for the Yellow Pages, which is a multi-billion dollar industry. He may not have said this if I were a man. Either way, it was another reminder that some people (even people from your own race) can't handle the idea of seeing you break with tradition. The same can be said of women who undercut other women. I have seen and experienced situations where women who have female bosses do things to make their boss look bad; and seen those same women be very supportive of male bosses.

Even now, as a semi-retired person, I encounter people who want to put road blocks up to keep me from doing something I want to do, take credit for something I've done, or talk down something I have done. There was a time in my life when people's responses to my being non-traditional really bothered me. In my late 20s and early 30s I even tried to be what I thought other people wanted me to be. But I found out two things:

- I wasn't good at being something I'm not.
- People didn't like me any better. In fact, I became a joke to them.

So I decided to be myself, and I've been happy ever since.

A big part of that happiness has come from deciding what I wanted from life and what I wanted to contribute to life. Once I figured that out, decision-making got easier. I also took an inventory of my life—looking at the blessings. Is *everything* exactly the way I want it to be? No. But when I add the pluses and subtract the minuses, the bottom line is a plus. I think that's pretty good. There are people who can't say that. So, even though being "different" is hard, the older I get the less concerned I am about it. I just try to enjoy the life I have and do what I can to make a difference in the world.

MIND GAMES

We are bombarded on a daily basis by messages from the media about what we should look like, what our lifestyle should be like, what we should wear, what we should like, what it means to be successful, who's cool and who's not. In our daily interaction with people we experience the same thing. People consciously and unconsciously try to:

- Mold us into what *they* think we should be like. For example, you may naturally be a quiet person. There's nothing wrong with that. But some people try to make you feel badly about yourself because you're not more outgoing or don't spend all your time hanging out.
- Determine what career you should choose by planting doubt in your mind about whether you can succeed in a "non-traditional" career. Some people will criticize your career choice, try to sow doubt in your mind about whether you can learn what you have to learn to get the job, or try to convince you no one will hire you.
- Get you to conform to *their* image of "cool." For example, you may prefer to dress more conservatively than others, like music that is different from the music others listen to, or like to read and learn. Because of this, some people will call you a nerd, hassle you or bully you. They may even spread rumors and lies about you.

- Make judgments about whether or not you're "down with the people" or trying to be something you're not based on *their* definition of what that means. For example, if you don't talk a certain way, if you hang out with people from other racial, cultural and ethnic groups as well as your own, if you enjoy a wide range of arts and culture—including those from other cultures—you may be accused of trying to be something you're not or abandoning "your people."

- Convince you to do things that could move your life in directions you never intended for it to go. For example, people may try to get you to drink or smoke (even if you're underage) or do drugs or have sex. If you say "no," they may call you a wimp or a prude or say "everybody else is doing it, what's up with you?"

Whether you're getting your information or ideas from the media or individuals or organizations or groups or institutions, you need to be aware that some (perhaps much) of what they are doing is playing mind games designed to shape your opinion and your actions.

I'm not suggesting you should *never* listen to what others have to say. No one knows it all. Others can and do have ideas that can help you achieve your life goals. Others can see problems and pitfalls you can't. But you should learn to think for yourself—to weigh and evaluate what others tell you. You should be comfortable being who you are. There are other people like you out there. There are people out there who are comfortable being around those who are not cookie-cutter duplicates of themselves. Find them and create your own social/professional network rather than try to make yourself fit into a group that's not broadminded enough to allow you to be yourself.

I also am not suggesting all media messages should be ignored. You can pick up valuable information from a wide variety of media sources. It's important to find out whether that information is coming from someone who really knows what they're talking about and is trying to give you a balanced view of what's going on, or whether it's coming from someone who has an agenda and will use half-truths and outright lies to convince you that what they're saying is true. You should cross-reference what you hear or read with information from more than one source so you can get a broader perspective about an issue or situation. When I say cross-reference, I mean make sure you're not just checking sources that agree with the way you think. Not everything in life is black or white, left or right, yes or no.

To make decisions for yourself, and determine what's real and what's propaganda, you need to develop critical thinking skills. You can develop these skills by:

- Researching the facts about an issue or situation for yourself rather than totally relying on what others tell you. People can tell you anything. They may think they're passing on good information, but often they're only repeating something they heard but did not verify. Some people may make up things because they're too embarrassed to say they don't know. Others may intentionally make things up to throw you off your game.
- Sorting through things you hear, see and read, and evaluating that information in terms of whether it will help, interfere with, or derail your chances of achieving your life goals.
- Learning whose advice to listen to and whose advice to ignore. Pay attention to who consistently gives you information or opinions that help you move toward your life goals. Using this standard will help you determine who you can trust. Even when you think you can trust what someone says, *do your own homework* when you're making a major, potentially life altering decision.
- Thinking about the short- and long-term consequences of your actions or decisions—what impact those actions will have on achieving your life goals; what positive and negative impacts your actions will have on other people's lives.
- Learning to play the game of chess. Chess teaches you to think before you make a move—a skill you can use in life to avoid pitfalls. It also teaches you to anticipate the moves of those who might try to block your progress so you can think *in advance* about how you will get around the obstacles they put up between you and your goals.
- Praying for guidance to do the right thing.

Thinking things through and praying for guidance will help you avoid a lot of the unproductive detours created by mind games.

Being Cool

Every generation comes up with a definition of what it means to be cool. That definition is reflected in music, dress, hairstyles and language. There is an element of rebellion in the tradition of being cool. Coolness pushes the envelope—meaning the cool people (who often are seen as the trendsetters and change agents) do things designed to make them different from others. Often because they are seen as rebels, they become popular, part of the "in crowd"—the people others try to imitate.

There is nothing inherently wrong with innovation and change. In fact, it's been said the only constant in the universe is change. Change is why we have indoor toilets instead of just outhouses. It is why we have electric lights instead of just candles to light our homes. It's why the laws of this country support equality instead of slavery and segregation.

But change is not always good. What's "cool" is not always good. In today's culture it's cool to walk around with an attitude—looking like you're mad at the world and ready to fight at the slightest insult (real or imagined). It's cool to use foul language in everyday conversations, even when children and the elderly are around. It's cool to put down women and make them feel their most important role is to be a sex object. It's cool to love the one you're with instead of having a committed relationship. Today's culture says what matters most is what you look like, not what your character is like. Today's culture says everybody is doing it (whatever "it" is), and if you're not doing "it," you're not cool.

Today's culture pushes taking drugs (legal and illegal) for everything—to put you to sleep/to wake you up; to help you remember/to help you forget; to help you lose weight/to help you gain weight; to help you feel young and vigorous/to prove to others you're grown. Today's culture makes it cool to pretend you're not academically gifted even if you are. Today's culture says it's cool to be a party animal and not cool if you're not. Today's culture makes it cool to do whatever it takes to get ahead in business, in government, in education, in life no matter what impact it has on others. Today's culture says the only cool careers are entertainment and sports.

I believe in another definition of cool. To me, being cool is not about going along with the latest fad or trend, it's about being who you are—an original. Really cool people define what's cool for them. It's a tougher definition of cool to pull off. Everyone wants to be popular, so it's easier to go with what's the "in" thing today. But since part of what it means to be cool is to go against the grain:

- Why not *start* a trend instead of following the most current one?
- Why not have people trying to be like you instead of you trying to be like everyone else?
- Instead of hiding your academic gifts, why not be the next Bill Gates who started Microsoft, or B. Smith who owns restaurants and a finer living lifestyle empire (like Martha Stewart)?
- Instead of focusing most of your attention on what you look like, why not spend equal time cultivating a beautiful personality, a kind spirit and a sharp, inquisitive mind?
- Instead of doing whatever it takes (right or wrong, legal or illegal, selfish or unselfish) to get ahead, why not focus on being honest and fair in your dealings with others?
- Instead of doing something because "everybody's doing it," why not decide what works for you—what you value most—and do that instead?

The people we read about in history books are not those who followed the trends, but those who set them. So be an original. Establish a new, positive trend by defining what cool is for you. In the long run you will get more out of life, and feel better about yourself.

IT TAKES A STRONG MAN TO BE GENTLE

The most common portrayal of manhood in American popular culture is the tough guy—the rugged individualist who doesn't smile, doesn't say much, doesn't show his feelings or who talks tough and takes no prisoners. These "tough guys" always have everything under control, never admit they're wrong, and are ready to fight any time, anywhere. That image is long standing and has been promoted in a variety of ways:

- **In print form:** through dime novels that were published beginning in 1860. The novels featured cowboys, gunfighters, hardboiled detectives such as Sam Spade, adventure stories or science fiction. The tough guy tradition continues today in urban fiction, also known as Street Lit' and Gangsta fiction.

- **In film:** through cowboy movies, gangster movies ranging from 1930s portrayals by actors such as Edward G. Robinson to the current urban gangsta films; and action-hero movies in which the main character is a one-man army who single-handedly takes on the world.

- **In music videos:** through portrayals of hard-edged guys who "don't take no stuff" from anybody; who talk about others like they don't have a right to exist; and who focus on the negative things going on in the world but don't offer any ideas for making things better for themselves or anyone else.

There is nothing wrong with being strong, assertive and competitive (as long as it's not a "do *anything* to win" type of competitiveness). But there's also nothing wrong with being kind, compassionate and gentle—even if you are a male. President Obama is a prime example of this. On the one hand, you don't get to be President of the United States by being a pushover. But even as he ran for office, he refused to get down in the gutter and sling dirt at his opponents to win. During the campaign to become President he met opposition, problems and attacks in a straight-forward, dignified, no-nonsense way, focusing on making sure attempts to distort his record or create and perpetuate lies about his message did not go unchallenged. When Republicans aired an ad during the campaign that attacked his wife, he said clearly during a news interview, "lay off my wife." As President he has not hesitated to make tough choices. For example his:

- Decision to do what was necessary to save a U.S. seaman from Somali pirates.
- Authorization to capture *or* kill Osama Bin Laden.
- Commitment to move his agenda forward (such as his comment "don't bet against me" during a news conference about his health care initiative and its chances of passing). When President Obama signed The Patient Protection and Affordable Care Act into law in 2010 he achieved what no other administration had before—beginning with Theodore Roosevelt who pushed for universal health coverage as a candidate for re-election to the office of President on the Progressive (Bull Moose) Party ticket in 1912.

On the gentler side, he holds hands with his wife and goes out on "date nights." He is affectionate to his children, and involved in their activities. He has no problem smiling.

I believe if you are comfortable with who you are, you don't have to always try to be intimidating and beat on your chest to make others respect you. When you're comfortable in your own skin, others will recognize that and give you your props.

DON'T MEASURE YOUR SUCCESS
BY SOMEONE ELSE'S LIFE

One of the surest ways to *not* get as much out of life as you want is to spend too much time comparing yourself to others. It's o.k. to look at someone who is doing something you want to do and learn from them. It's another thing to obsess over *why* someone is getting an opportunity you're not getting, or *why* their lives are "so much better" than yours.

We're all put here on earth by God to do what *He* wants us to do. The key to success in life, in my opinion, is to find out what your purpose is, and put your energy there. It took me a while to figure this out. But one day when I was complaining to myself about what I didn't have that I wanted, this thought crossed my mind: Take a look at what you *do* have. I did, and I can truly say I wouldn't trade my life for anyone else's—not because every minute of every day has been happy and carefree, or because everything in my life turned out the way I wanted it to. But when I add up the pluses and the minuses, the bottom line is a big plus. I'm able to provide for my basic needs—food, clothing and shelter. I have my family. I have my health. I'm able to do things I enjoy doing—travel, attend sports, arts and cultural events. (I have to budget to do these things, but I still can do them.) I have people with whom I can do things I enjoy. I have most of the "things" I want in life. With all these pluses, for me to view my life as anything but successful would be the height of ingratitude.

To keep myself from making negative comparisons to others, I try on a daily basis to remember and appreciate what I have. I admit that sometimes I still forget how blessed I am. When that happens, I "do the math" again to remind myself about all the pluses in my life. Focusing on those pluses and trying to be the best person I can be leaves less time to spend comparing myself to others.

So my advice to those who want to live an enjoyable life is to focus on doing what you can do to the best of your ability, and appreciate what you have. Wasting time measuring your success against someone else's will only make you miserable, and increase the amount of time it takes you to create the type of life and lifestyle you want.

GOD DON'T MAKE NO JUNK

There is no such thing as a worthless human being. Everyone on the planet was put here for a special purpose. Sometimes things happen to people—usually hurtful comments or actions—that make them feel worthless. Sometimes that hurt is so deep they think it's impossible to heal their spirit. But their spirit can be healed through acts of kindness and caring that lets them know God don't make no junk. Before acting all high and mighty and passing judgment on someone remember, there but for the grace of God go you.

If you are blessed to be in a situation where hope is still alive and well in your spirit, make sure you support non-profit organizations that serve individuals in need with your time, talent or treasure. Even more importantly make sure you support non-profit organizations that work to prevent people from reaching the point where they are in dire need. Take time to be a mentor to a younger person who, with your help, is willing to do what it takes to move beyond his or her immediate circumstances.

Those who are under 18-years-old don't have to wait until they are an adult who is established in their career to do this. You can "adopt" a little sister or brother from your neighborhood or your school. If you look around you'll notice younger people watching you to see what you're doing. They will follow your lead and your example. Include them in positive activities that help expand their view of what is possible in the world. Connect them with caring positive adults from your family, church, the community center, youth programs, school.

Mentor a friend or acquaintance your age who may be going through a difficult time.

If each of us reaches back to help even one person, we can have a significant impact on changing the world for the better. When one person's life is put on a more positive footing, that allows them to help someone else. Like the waves created when a stone is thrown into the water, one life turned around can have a ripple affect on the lives of many others.

If you are in a situation where hope is fading, reach out for help before hope dies. Connect with someone at school, church, the community center or someone in your extended family or in the family of one of your friends who can offer support and help you move your life in a positive direction. Look for people who are making it out of the chaos you may be living in and ask them to help you. You may not succeed in getting help on the first try, but keep trying. Someone will give you a hand up. Don't give up. Remember: God don't make no junk.

Love Yourself First

If you are going to be a positive force in the world, it is important to love yourself first. I'm not talking about the conceited kind of love where you think the world revolves around you. Rather, I'm talking about the kind of self love where you feel good about who you are as a person. Self love is important for two reasons:

- It gives you more control over your life.
- It is hard to love and care for someone else if you don't love and care for yourself.

Gaining Control Over Your Life

Too many people rely on other people to make them feel good about themselves. They:

- Spend much of their time trying to be what someone else wants them to be.
- Let others talk them into doing things they don't feel comfortable doing just to make the other person happy. Often this leads to destructive decisions that can kill dreams, create unnecessary hardships and destroy promising lives (such as drug or alcohol addiction, parenthood without the resources to properly take care of a child, mental depression, sickness or

injury, long-term health problems, and illegal activities that can lead to imprisonment).

- Try to "buy their friendship" by spending money on gifts, entertainment, clothes—whatever will make the *other* person "happy."

If you don't feel good about yourself, others can manipulate you. For example:

- People in abusive relationships often have low self-esteem. Because they may not have fully learned to love themselves first and recognize they are worthy of better treatment, the abuser is able to manipulate their feelings in a way that keeps them in that unhealthy relationship.
- Those who are bullied and have or develop low self-esteem can become depressed and (in extreme cases) may try to harm themselves up to and including suicide.
- People can be convinced they are not capable of achieving their goals in life, and give up on their dreams.

Counting on others to make you feel good about yourself does not work in the long run. More times than not, those who jerk your life around like a puppet on a string won't like you any better just because you do what they want. What usually happens if you allow them to manipulate you is that you end up paying a high emotional price. In addition to developing doubts about yourself and your self-worth, you may find yourself on an emotional roller coaster—feeling good about yourself one day and bad the next day.

God puts each one of us here to carry out a mission that only we can fulfill. The cornerstone for self love is finding out what that mission is and focusing on carrying it out. To do this you have to define *your* values—the rules *you* want to live by—and stick with them.

Now, I'm not saying you should never listen to ideas or suggestions from others. Sometimes God helps us do what he wants us to do by speaking through others.

Sometimes people can see potential in us that we can't see in ourselves. What they see can help us become better people. But before you start doing a complete makeover, ask yourself:

- Is this something I would tell someone I really care about to do?
- Is this something that will help me get where I want to be in life?

- Five years from now, will doing this make me feel better or worse about my life?
- What impact will my doing this have on others—particularly those I care about?
- If what I do makes the news, how would I feel about that?

Caring About Others

The second reason that loving yourself is important is this: if you are unhappy with yourself, subconsciously you want others to be unhappy, too. There's an old saying: *misery loves company.* Even if you don't *intend* to do so, when you are miserable you do things to make others miserable. Also, when you are unhappy about yourself you are so focused on *you* that you are less aware of the needs of others. Therefore, you're less likely to do things that will help others (which, ultimately, is what we're all put here to do in various ways).

I am convinced that love is the most powerful force on earth. But before that power can be unleashed in the world, we have to love ourselves first.

BEAUTY COMES FROM WITHIN

There's such an emphasis on looks in our society that it seems to overshadow everything else. We have become so wrapped up in the culture of beauty, celebrity and wearing the right brands that we have lost sight of the things that really matter: being honest and trustworthy, being dependable and faithful, having good manners and treating people the way you would like to be treated (with respect and caring), developing your talents and gifts and putting them to good use for yourself *and* others, being kind, considerate and pleasant to be around.

People who are focused on whether they look good and wear the right brands often go for "the look" without thinking about what really looks good on them. They want to dress and wear their hair like their favorite celebrity, even though that look might not work for their body type and face. Even if they achieve "the look," the way they walk, sit, talk, eat, and speak does not always reflect the sophistication they are trying to convey.

Now, don't get me wrong. I firmly believe in doing whatever I can to look my best. If fact, I took a modeling class when I was growing up to learn about choosing the style of clothing that looks best on *my* body, the colors that look best with *my* skin and hair color, how to mix and match colors, designs and fabrics and how to walk, stand and sit gracefully. Taking this class helped me develop my own style and look, and taught me how to upgrade that look as fashions changed while still being me. Having said this, I still believe the emphasis on external beauty is short sighted for a number of reasons:

- An accident or illness can take that beauty away in a moment.
- What's "in" today can be "out" tomorrow. Sometimes "big" women are in. Other times "skinny" women or "buff" women are in.
- Trying to keep up with changes and the "competition" (other women) can easily become a full-time job. You can spend a lot of time and money making yourself over. And, after all is said and done, things still may not work out the way you want them to because beauty is in the eye of the beholder. The "beholder" you may have *your* eye on may have a different definition of beauty than what you have to offer.
- "New models" are coming on the market everyday. As we get older, our tight bodies will start to soften and sag. Even if we do everything we can to keep in shape, we can't count on competing on the basis of looks with those who are 10, 20, 30 or more years younger than we are.
- Spending hard-earned cash on keeping up with people whose paychecks may be significantly larger than ours means that current and future needs (like education for ourselves and our children, and retirement) may not be taken care of. This live-in-the moment approach almost assures that life will be less comfortable and enjoyable when we get older.

So, while it may seem that cultivating the body, hair, clothes and "look" is the most important thing, that approach is shortsighted. When looks fade, you could face a lonely, isolated old age if other qualities that make you attractive are not there. People eventually get tired of ugly ways. As we get older, most people start paying more attention to who a person "really is" (what makes them pleasant or unpleasant to be around) rather than what they look like. The beauty that comes from being your best self lasts longer than any physical beauty. That's why I believe the primary focus should be on cultivating the beauty within—those things that will stand the test of time:

- Kindness.
- Respect and caring for others.
- Honesty, trustworthiness and dependability.

- Developing your God-given talents in a way that not only benefits you but also makes the world a better place.
- Maintaining an intellectual curiosity that encourages you to grow, develop and continue learning. This will make you a more interesting person because you are willing to participate in a wide variety of activities, and can carry on a good conversation on a wide range of topics.

Focusing on *these* things has a lasting positive impact on your life and the lives of those you come in contact with. It makes a lifetime of real beauty and good living achievable.

BEING BI-CULTURAL

It sounds like a cliché but it's true: the world is shrinking. Even small towns in this country are starting to experience cultural diversity, as are European countries. While every country has its dominant culture—its standard way of doing things and standard beliefs and values—I believe every culture has value. Having said that, the trick for those who are not members of the dominant culture is to maintain their unique cultural values and identity while functioning effectively within the dominant culture.

If you want to achieve your dreams and you're not a member of the dominant culture, you have to learn to navigate your way through that culture. Doing this involves being aware of such things as what is considered proper dress, speech and behavior in your school, work, and social environment.

Some people consider doing this "selling out." I disagree. I call it being bi-cultural. What do I mean by that? Let me use an example that is more obvious. When I went to Senegal, West Africa in the 1980s I had never traveled to a predominately Muslim country before. The trip with a group of artists was during Ramadan—the high holy period for Muslims. I did some homework to become familiar with what was and was not acceptable in terms of dress and behavior. I learned that women were expected to be modest in their dress. Based on that, I made myself a whole wardrobe of tunic tops and pants out of light-weight gauzy material that would allow me to have my arms and legs appropriately covered, but would not be too hot for weather conditions. That decision helped me enjoy my time in Senegal while still being respectful of the country's values. Whenever I travel to another country I also try to learn some of the language so I can at least make an attempt to speak to people in their native tongue. I have found that just trying to speak their language is enough to get people to respond to me in a more friendly and helpful way. Just as adjusting to differences when you travel outside this country isn't "selling out," neither is adjusting to cultural differences *within* this country.

I believe making adjustments is a skill that has been lost in recent years, but can be learned. People of color like me who grew up in this country during segregation and the modern civil rights era learned this skill. As *legal* racial barriers fell and more opportunities opened up for us, we adapted to the desegregated environment and learned to navigate in whatever circumstances we found ourselves (which helped us take advantage of new opportunities). At the same time, we maintained our ties to the community and to our cultural heritage. We learned how to fit in without losing our true selves. For example, I dress in a manner that is appropriate for where I'm going. If the dress code for work is a suit and dress shoes, that's what I wear. When I go to church, I dress differently from the way I dress when I'm running around doing errands. Other examples: my favorite forms of music are jazz, R&B *and* classical. I enjoy the plays of August Wilson and Lorraine Hansberry as well as Eugene O'Neill and Arthur Miller. I can speak standard ("correct") English as well as Ebonics. A short story to illustrate this last point: When I was a newspaper reporter in Miami, one of the paper's prize-winning veteran reporters (who happened to be white) asked another African American reporter (Bea Hines) and me to listen to the tape of an African American woman he had interviewed and tell him what she was saying. He was working on a book, and was having trouble understanding some of the things she said. Bea (who also speaks standard English) and I had no trouble understanding the woman, translated her Ebonics, and gave our colleague the information he needed. He thanked us both in the book's acknowledgments.

Being bi-cultural doesn't mean cutting yourself off from other members of your cultural or ethnic group. When I was growing up, my family was a middle-income version of the *Cosby Show*. We were not unique. Two-parent families where both husband and wife worked were the norm. The adults in those families set standards, instilled discipline in their children, made sure children got a good education so they could take their place in society as responsible and productive adults, and passed on family traditions. One of my family's traditions is to give back—to do what I can to help others. A lot of our giving back is to people who share my cultural heritage largely because that is where the greatest need is.

Again, my family is not unique. There are any number of African American organizations and individuals who give their time, talent and treasure to help others move up. They have positions of authority in organizations and companies. Many (like me) have opened doors for business and employment opportunities for those who had previously been shut out. They work or volunteer every day to achieve social and economic justice. They may not dress in the latest celebrity styles. They may not even live in the heart of the city. But they are, nonetheless, still connected to the community. They continue to be proud of who they are as they swim in the big pond of the dominant culture. In short, they regularly demonstrate it is possible to be bi-cultural without being a "sell-out." There are a number of benefits to being bi-cultural:

- **It keeps you grounded.** Every culture throughout history has contributed something of value to human civilization. Knowing your history—appreciating *and* feeling good about who you are, where you came from, and the traditions that make you different from someone else—helps protect your mind and spirit from the attacks of those who would claim that only *their* group has ever done anything worth while; or who would say that your traditions are somehow inferior to theirs. While I like more tailored clothing, I frequently accessorize with Afro-centric jewelry or scarves or bright colors. If you visit my home, my art, books and music collection leave no doubt about what my cultural background is.

- **You feel comfortable in different settings** because you have learned how to handle yourself in a variety of environments.

- **It helps you achieve your life goals.** While it doesn't knock down all barriers, knowing how things are done in the dominant culture helps you know what to expect and how to play the game. Life to me is like the board game chess. If you want to win the game (or at least be competitive) you have to anticipate the moves your opponent will make. If you know the rules of the dominant culture's game, study people's behavior and actions to learn what they do in various situations, and get an understanding of what motivates those actions, you develop the ability to make decisions and take actions that increase the likelihood you will achieve your dreams.

- **It gives you experiences you might not otherwise have had**, which can move your career or personal life in unexpected positive directions. I learned about investing in the stock market on my first job. I may have heard of stocks and bonds, but I didn't have experience with them or discussions about them when I was growing up—even though my parents were highly educated and my grandparents were business people. Learning about investing helped me not only live more comfortably than my salary would otherwise have allowed, but also helped me retire from the workforce early, while maintaining a comfortable lifestyle.

- **It adds variety and spice to life by making you more willing to try new things.** I would argue that a lot of us are bi- or multi-cultural already without knowing it. We eat foods from different cultures: pizza, chicken, tacos, spaghetti, egg rolls. We listen to music rooted in different cultures. We play and watch sports that come from different cultures: basketball, golf, tennis, soccer, bowling, football. We use slang terms from other cultures: trippin', chutzpa, dis. We wear clothes and jewelry based on styles and color schemes from different cultures: African, French, Italian, Asian, Hispanic. The fact is each of us in the United States (where so many different cultures have interacted with each other for centuries) really have more in common than we think. Therefore, we can all be proud of who we are *and* where we came from.

There is no reason for anyone to be afraid to, reluctant to, or bullied into refusing to learn the skills and cultural norms necessary to successfully function within the dominant culture. If you need *proof* this approach can work, think about the family that moved into the White House on January 20, 2009.

CELEBRATE YOUR CULTURAL ROOTS, HONOR OTHERS'

In the 1980s I took a trip to Senegal, West Africa with the National Conference of Black Artists. I heard about the trip from a talented and accomplished local visual artist, Gerald Duane Coleman. Going to visit my cultural homeland had always been a dream, so I jumped at the opportunity.

When we arrived at the airport in Dakar, the capital city, we were greeted by drummers, dancers, and stilt walkers decked out in traditional clothing. As we walked through the welcome line one of the greeters shouted, "Welcome American cousins!" It caught me off guard for a moment. Even though I was born in Crystal Springs, MS, grew up in Milwaukee, WI, and certainly considered myself an American, it surprised me that people from the continent from which my ancestors came saw me first as American rather than African. That was the first of many "aha" moments I would have during my 10-day stay on the continent.

I'm a people watcher—probably a direct outgrowth of the fact that I'm a recovering shy person. Shy people tend to spend more time watching what's going on around them than talking. Throughout the time I was in Senegal I kept seeing things that looked familiar to me. I remember seeing people standing in small groups talking with each other and gesturing not just with their hands but with their bodies—the way I have seen Black people doing all my life back home. In casual settings among friends in the U.S., when a Black person is telling a story or making a point, frequently you'll see his or her head and body moving for emphasis.

In our orientation at the hotel before our first trip to the marketplace our tour guide told us that bargaining for a better price was part of West African tradition, so we shouldn't accept the first price offered. He told us even if the seller seemed to be getting agitated, keep bargaining and even walk away. He said bargaining is not only the norm, but it is considered an important part of the social process. To buy something without a good stiff negotiation to get the "best price" was not considered good form. Whatever price they give you after you walk away is likely their best price, he said. As an American that was a new concept for me, but I managed to get into the swing of it—until the last day of the trip. I was tired and only made a half-hearted attempt at negotiating the price of an item I wanted. When I said o.k. too soon the woman I was making the purchase from got this hurt look on her face. She took my money but added another item to my purchase, which she did not charge me for. I felt bad that I had broken the social contract.

The bargaining experience in Senegal reminded me of how often as a business owner in the U.S. I have Black people trying to talk me down on the price of my marketing services, even though I know my prices are among the lowest in town. This bargaining wasn't just done by those with modest budgets. Even people I *know* have money try to negotiate. A fellow business owner referred to this tendency as a "black tax." She said African Americans rarely "negotiate" price with people of other nationalities the way they do with Black-owned businesses. Her theory is that this is a carry over from slavery and "Jim Crow" (legalized segregation) when African Americans were repeatedly reminded by words, actions, and laws that they were not as valuable nor had the same rights as those in the dominant culture. She said this attitude was probably subconsciously passed on to future generations of African Americans who continue to devalue the work of members of their own cultural group. Psychologists and sociologists have done studies on the impact inequality has on people that suggest she could be right. My experience in Senegal opened up an additional possibility: Black people today are predisposed to bargaining because previous generations more closely connected to the West African civilizations from which most African Americans are descended may have passed on this tradition to their descendants.

Another "aha" moment occurred on a tour where we were entertained by singers who used the call and response style in which the song leader would chant the words and the rest of the group would respond by singing the words back—a style that is characteristic of traditional Negro Spirituals.

A truly impactful part of the trip came when we visited Goree Island, the final shipping point for slaves to the Americas. Our guide—a small, slender, dark-skinned man who spoke in a soft voice—told us in unflinching detail the story of what life in "The Castle" was like for the captives. Then he took us to the "Door of No Return"—the small slit in the wall through which the captives, one by one, stepped to board the ships that would take them to a harsh life in an unknown part of the world. Our guide then left us there to soak it all in. His understated dignified manner reminded me of the way members of my grandparents' generation carried themselves. Despite growing up and living in segregated conditions, they maintained a quiet but unmistakable dignity about themselves, and a determination to create the best possible life for themselves and their children.

One of the biggest "aha" moments came when we went to a performance of Senegal's national dance company. The dances were in the West African tradition that I expected to see—until the last one. Two men who appeared to be in their 50s came out and started doing a dance in which they spun around on their backs, rippled their arms in a wave-like fashion, spun around on their heads and did other moves that looked exactly like break dancing. I was startled. As I left the theatre I asked one of our hosts about the dance. Not wanting to offend, I said "Tell me about that last dance. It looks very much like what we call break dancing in the United States." He smiled and said, "Oh no. That's a traditional dance called the Juggler's Dance. It's hundreds of years old." At that point it hit me that African American young people in the United States who had never been to Africa were, nevertheless, doing something their ancestors had done centuries before on another continent. I wondered whether that skill and knowledge was transmitted through their DNA.

After I returned from that trip, I was asked by a publisher's representative to write a book in a series entitled *Cultures of America*. The book, aimed at middle-school children, focused on identifying those traditions from their cultural homeland that Americans passed down from generation to generation. In addition to the information I found through research, I included some of the stories and experiences from my trip to Africa to illustrate how the traditions continued. What these two experiences—the trip and writing the book—really brought home to me was (perhaps more than any other place on the planet) the United States really is a microcosm of the world. My nationality is

American—something I am very proud of and would not change. My cultural heritage is both African and American. I am proud of, embrace and celebrate both parts of that heritage. Each of us has a right to do the same.

These experiences also brought into clearer focus the importance of some of the stories I had been hearing from my parents throughout my life. I remember a story my father told me about a flu outbreak when he was a child. It hit his hometown of Forest, MS hard. Many of the Caucasian residents in the town became seriously ill or died. However, few residents of African ancestry did. My father explained Black people went out in the woods, picked leaves from a particular plant and boiled them to produce "fever tea." The tea warded off the effects of the flu. Today, a growing number of doctors trained in the Western medical tradition are starting to pay more attention to and use herbal medicines and home remedies. Acupuncture—an eastern (Chinese) medical tradition that was belittled when it was first introduced in this country—is increasingly accepted.

Each culture brings something of value to the table. Each culture contributes to the advancement and richness of human life. Each culture has had its good times and its bad times. We should each celebrate every part of who we are culturally as well as nationally, and recognize that no one culture is superior or inferior to another.

JUST BE YOURSELF

Each of us is a one-of-a-kind original. We have our own personalities, our own place in the universal order, our own purpose in life. God made us unique. He threw away the mold after He made us, so we should celebrate who we are rather than complain because we are not like someone else.

There is tremendous pressure everyday to conform to a narrow definition of what's "in." There are societal standards of beauty, dress and behavior that may or may not fit you or be to your benefit. For example, you may decide not to do your best in school because you don't want others to think you're not cool. However, in a world where knowledge and brain power are the keys to a comfortable lifestyle, such a choice means you are limiting your career choices as an adult to low-wage jobs.

If you decide to hang with a fast crowd, chances are good you'll end up getting into some kind of trouble that could derail your dreams for a bright future. That derailment may come because you don't get serious about preparing yourself to be financially self-sufficient as an adult, or it may come because you do something illegal and have a criminal record that makes it harder for you to get the job or career you want.

If you decide to do whatever it takes to "get" someone you're attracted to, you may find yourself in a relationship where you are constantly doing what they want to "keep" them (even if it's something you'd rather not do). This relationship could become abusive. It could also result in parenthood at a time when you don't have the financial or emotional resources to raise a child in a way that will help him or her become a positive, productive adult.

Before I go any further, I want to make it clear when I talk about being yourself, I'm *not* talking about being a total maverick—an "it's my way or the highway" type of person. In society there are rules and standards that we must abide by if we are to live together in harmony. We can't steal, kill, lie, cheat, run red lights, or do things that hurt another person just because we feel like it. There has to be a balance between societal norms and individuality. If we want to advance in our careers, there are concessions we have to make. For example you can't dress like you're going to the beach if you work in an office or a food or retail outlet. You have to show up regularly, on time, and do a good job if you want to keep your job. You can't get someone "told" on the job every time they do something you don't like. (You can raise an issue with them, but it needs to be done in a low volume, professional way with documentation to make your case. If that doesn't work, you can take your case to the next level in the company for review, or seek outside legal assistance.)

With these limitations in mind, I still say trying to be something you're not will not only lead to disappointment and, often, failure, but also doesn't make you happy. When you're not yourself, you have to constantly be on guard to remember how you're *supposed* to act, look, etc. It's like trying to remember a lie. When you tell the story the next time it's going to be different, and someone will catch you not being truthful. That's stressful.

I'm a nerd. I always have been one. From grade school on I've been one of those people who always had her head in a book. I love learning. That was not a good thing when I was growing up. I had people who would give me a hard time because I was a bookworm. On top of that I was shy.

When I graduated from high school and went to college, I thought I'd try becoming a "new" me. My first semester in college I went to parties and found that alcohol (one drink) made me sick. Some students at parties I attended smoked marijuana. I didn't, and didn't feel comfortable being around them when they broke out the weed. So, I'd leave the party. Some students put partying higher on their priority list than studying. That didn't work for me. So, ultimately, I found myself right back where I fit in best—hanging with the nerds on campus. Looking back, I'm glad it worked out that way. Not only did I feel more comfortable with myself and my surroundings, but I was also able to focus more on what I really wanted, and create a life I'm happy with.

Today I'm more comfortable with being myself than ever. I don't feel embarrassed by or feel a need to hide my love of nerdy stuff. My radio dial is set on National Public Radio—not the top hits station. On television I mainly watch news and information programs and sports. I love many kinds of music—jazz, classical, R & B and some country and western. I love books. I love the arts—theatre, dance, visual. I have networks of people with similar interests that I get together with to share these interests. I'm a big sports fan, and have a "family" of people I enjoy being with. (Some of them work at sporting events I attend and some attend those events.) I can laugh, talk, *and* feel sorry with them when the team doesn't do well. I'm a classic/conservative dresser—not someone who tries to look like a Hollywood starlet. As I've grown older, I've noticed I'm getting more and more compliments for my "look."

I still run into people who want to fit me into *their* box. But I've learned deciding which box *I* want to fit in is a less stressful way to live.

TAKING CARE OF YOU

Your Body is Your Temple, Take Care of It

You only get one body in life. To make it last and keep it healthy for as long as possible, you have to take care of it. That means doing all the things you always hear about: eating properly; getting exercise to maintain your proper weight and keep your muscles, heart and joints in shape; drinking enough water; reducing stress; getting enough sleep; and not putting substances in your body that will harm you.

It all sounds simple but, given the frantic pace most of us keep, it's not as easy as it sounds. But it can be done. Like anything else you're really committed to achieving, you have to be intentional about taking care of your body. That means you have to:

- Pay attention to what you eat, including snacks.
- Look for ways to get your body moving and your heart pumping, whether it's walking up stairs rather than taking an elevator, riding a bike or walking to places that are not too far away instead of riding in a car.
- Drink the water in the bottle you carry around all day rather than just carry the bottle.
- Make time for yourself to do things you enjoy at least three or four times a week (if not every day) to keep your spirits up.

- Turn off the television and record a show you want to see rather than stay up to watch it when you have to get up early the next day.
- Avoid drugs and other substances that can harm your body.

The life expectancy in the United States right now is 78-years-old. If you're not in good health, that can feel like a long time.

Even if you haven't done a good job of taking care of your body in the past, it's not too late. Now is the best time to change what you're doing. It will make a world of difference in your qualify of life as you grow older.

CHOOSE LIFE

Death is inevitable. At some point we are all going to die. But the choices we make in life can speed up the death clock.

If you're driving 100 miles an hour when the speed limit is 55, · you're increasing the likelihood you'll miss a curve and crash. Speed limits aren't there to annoy drivers. They are an indication that the road was built to be driven safely up to that speed.

If you drink while under the legal age, you're doing damage to your developing body. That could impact your health in the future. If you drink and drive, you run the risk of injuring or killing yourself or someone else. If you drink to get drunk you are destroying your body.

If your primary food intake is junk food or high-fat fast food, you don't exercise, and you don't get enough rest, you increase the risk of diseases that will cause your body to break down faster than if you eat a balanced diet, and get the rest and exercise you need to stay healthy.

If you abuse drugs (prescription or illegal) you set yourself up for both a physical and living death. Physical death can be the result of an overdose, murder because you're in the wrong place at the wrong time, a traffic accident while driving under the influence or some other accident. Living death can come from spending your life doing whatever it takes (regardless of legality) to feed your habit and (often times) living in or spending a lot of time in rundown, unsafe environments. Living death could also mean wasting away in a prison cell where your nearly every move is dictated by someone else, and the opportunities for living a comfortable, productive life (even if you get out of jail) are significantly diminished. Employers are often reluctant to hire felons. Certain careers may be closed to you. You may lose your right to vote. Being a felon doesn't mean you are doomed to failure. But it *will* make success that much harder to achieve.

If you sleep around with different people you run the risk of contracting fatal or chronic sexually transmitted diseases that can shorten your life or cause you to have health problems the rest of your life. You also run the risk of having a child you may not be financially or emotionally able to support.

Life is precious, and it is short enough. The older you get, the more you realize how much more there is you would like to do, and how little time there is to do it all. Given a choice between what to do and what not to do, choose those things that will help you live longer and be healthier and more productive, *not* things that will shorten your life and make it more difficult.

In other words, choose life.

NATURAL HIGH

Taking drugs or getting drunk to alter your state of mind is something you don't need to do. Whatever it is you are trying to escape from will still be there when you sober up. Whatever you are searching for through an artificial high can be appreciated more if you aren't stoned. People will try to tell you differently. Don't believe them.

If you want to find peace and contentment in life, seek joy, not happiness. Happiness relies on external factors you don't always have control over—people, changes in your life circumstances, material possessions As those things change, how you feel about yourself and your life changes.

On the other hand, joy comes from within. You control your joy by the way you view and deal with whatever life hands you. Joy is organic. It becomes part of who you are and makes you more resilient—able to get through tough times and bounce back from whatever life throws at you.

Joy can help you make it through days when nothing seems to go right, by reminding you that things have, can and will get better if you just hang in there.

Joy can help you deal with troublesome schoolmates. In the workplace, joy can help you deal with bad bosses, co-workers or customers until you can find a better work environment or start your own business.

Joy can help you find meaning in less than desirable situations by focusing your attention on the lessons those situations are trying to teach you. Heeding those lessons will help you *not* repeat the same mistake.

Joy can help you face disappointment. Yes, you will feel sad or frustrated when things don't go your way. But joy will help you rebound—pick yourself up and move on with your life—because you know God only wants to give you the best in life. What you think you've lost will pale in comparison to what He has in store for you.

Joy will help you forgive those who do things to make you feel bad, keep you from succeeding, or bring you down. That forgiveness will keep you from being consumed by the need for revenge, the need to figure out why someone did what they did, or the need to spend time trying to make them "like" you (all of which interfere with your ability to focus on and achieve your true purpose in life).

Joy can help you fill that empty space when you lose a loved one by remembering the good times and remembering the struggles you overcame together.

Joy is a natural high so strong that nothing on earth can bring your spirit crashing to the ground. Given a choice between an artificial high that dumps you back into the same pit of problems after the high wears off, and the natural high of joy that helps you deal with and overcome those problems, choose joy.

Garbage In, Garbage Out

The data you put into a computer affects the value and truth of the information you get out of the computer. The phrase used to describe this is "garbage in, garbage out." Proverbs 23:7 in the Kings James version of the Bible puts it another way: "For as he thinketh in his heart, so is he."

The idea underlying both statements is the same: if you fill your mind with negative ideas you tend to think negative thoughts. That makes it more likely you will become a negative person, act in negative ways, and create a life that is less productive and satisfying than it could have been. If the music you listen to and videos you watch are filled with anger, hopelessness, negative attitudes about life and the world, and negative images about women, then your mind will likely see the world through the lens of anger, hopelessness, and negativity. Your image of who you are and what your life *can be* will be limited.

If you listen to and believe people who tell you what you *can't* do, you're less likely to follow your dreams, and less likely to work to become the best person you *can* be.

If you buy into the idea that all that matters is what *you* want, and that it's o.k. to lie, cheat and steal to get it, then you will likely miss opportunities to help others, which can give you a sense of joy and fulfillment that is better than anything you can get by being totally self-centered.

If you are not willing to roll up your sleeves and get involved in a positive way to oppose injustice, then you will miss the opportunity to make a positive difference in the quality of life for yourself, your family and your community.

To live your life to the fullest it is important to think about possibilities, and to believe you can make those possibilities happen. American scholar, author, editor, pastor and teacher William Arthur Ward put it this way: "If you can imagine it, you can achieve it; if you can dream it, you can become it."

Don't fill your mind with garbage. Fill it with things that are honest, true, pure, just and uplifting. By doing this, your life will be more satisfying, productive and worthwhile.

You're Only as Old as
You Think You Are

As of this writing I am 63 years old. But I don't get up in the morning thinking "I'm 63." I get up thinking "I'm Shelia."

We live in a culture where anyone over the age of 40 is considered over the hill, totally out of touch with what's happening and totally useless when it comes to telling anyone under that age anything that would be useful.

The idea that older people are relics from the past isn't new. I remember looking around at some other founding members of the Student Afro-American Society during a 25th anniversary ceremony in 1995 at Syracuse University. I thought we looked pretty good. Then I looked out at the audience of current students who had gathered for the ceremony. The look on their faces said, "I didn't know people lived to be that old." It made me laugh.

For many "seasoned" people, the emphasis on youth in our culture is a reason for them to try their best to deny the inevitable—that they are getting older. Some people spend lots of money trying to look younger than they are. They don't want to tell you how old they are. They dress like someone half their age.

I don't focus on my age. The alternative to getting older is to be dead, and that has no appeal. Instead, I focus on doing something useful, something I enjoy, and something that will make a difference in the world each day I'm on the planet. I also try to keep physically and mentally active. I don't exercise in a gym, but I try to make sure I get some walking in every day by parking my car at least two blocks away from where I need to go (instead of parking in the garage near the building). I walk up stairs whenever I can. And I engage, in a limited way, in sports. I watch my diet and try (less successfully, but I'm working on doing better) to make sure I get enough rest.

I keep my mind active by reading, writing, listening to public radio, and watching television (especially news and public affairs programs). I look for opportunities to learn new things. I set goals for myself—things I want to achieve—which gives me a reason to get up in the morning. In fact, I recently wrote down some of those goals—some personal, and some career. I do volunteer work. I find people who share my interests and spend time with them. I travel several times a year—usually to places I have not been before—so I can see more of the country and the world, and learn both how people are different and how we are alike.

I believe the key to staying young is to stay engaged in life. The moment you cut yourself off from the world, you truly begin to age.

It's been said that age is a number, and it is. That number has both an upside and a downside. On the down side of getting older:

- You can't burn the candle at both ends for as long as you used to.
- Despite your best efforts, things begin to sag and bulge.
- Physical changes may limit your ability to do some things you use to do.
- The older you are, the closer you are to the end of life.

But on the up side:

- You've seen and done enough to see the potholes in life *before* you hit them.
- You've learned the difference between what is worth worrying about and what isn't worth getting a pimple over.
- You don't feel you have to *prove* anything to anyone.
- You are freer to do things you like to do—you're not limited to doing things you *have* to do.
- You don't have to spend a lot of time around people you don't like.

I've seen some pretty old 20-year-olds and some pretty young 102-year-olds. As for me, I plan to follow the example of the lively 102-year-old.

Smiles Are Good for Your Health

I don't know how I developed this habit, but I smile a lot. When I walk down the street and make eye contact with someone (even someone I don't know) I'll smile. Most times they'll smile back and often speak. Even when I'm around the house by myself, I'll find myself laughing and smiling about something. Smiling makes me feel better. If I'm having a bad day, I try to find something to smile about. The way I know it's time to take a vacation or take a break from what I'm doing is that I stop smiling.

Things happen in life that can pluck your last nerve. So you can't smile all the time. But being in a regular state of anger or upset is bad for your health. Scientists have determined that feeling better when you smile is not just a psychological thing, it is also physical. When you smile your body releases chemicals called endorphins that make you not only feel better, but also play a role in healing your body and keeping you healthy. Negative thoughts, on the other hand, release enzymes and chemicals that tear down your body. So, you can see why it is important to keep the positive thoughts going as much as possible. The easiest way to do that is to smile.

I know smiling isn't always easy. When smiling is the last thing I feel like doing, I've learned to play a mental game with myself—I try to find the humor in a situation. One "game" when things are getting totally ridiculous is to step back mentally, look at everything that is not working, and say, "This is just ridiculous," and smile or laugh.

Another way to get past being grumpy is to look at the situation as if it's a comedy routine you might see on television or in a movie—one in which a clumsy person who is trying to be cool keeps bumping into things and knocking things over. Thinking about that scene makes me smile.

Another game I play with myself is to just stop and say, "O.k. I'm having a bad day. Tomorrow has *got* to be better than this," and smile.

I may ask myself "is this worth getting a pimple over?" Usually, the answer is "no," so I smile and move on.

If someone is annoying me, I may look at them like they're crazy, shake my head, and walk away. It totally throws them off, and it frees me from that annoying situation.

Each person has to identify what makes *them* smile, and use that to release the internal tension they are feeling.

The bottom line in dealing with life's ups and downs is to recognize you can't always control what is going on in your day, but you can control your reaction to it. I think the best reaction is to find the humor in the situation and smile—realizing that as long as you're inhaling air, things *can* get better.

So even when you don't feel like it, remember to smile. You will feel better, and live healthier.

Be Thankful for What You Have

If you listen to the world, happiness is about having "more" and having the "latest and greatest" stuff. Bling is what really counts. If you don't have it, if you're not living the celebrity lifestyle, you can't be happy.

It's not true.

Don't get me wrong. There is nothing wrong with having nice things. There's nothing wrong with being able to do things you enjoy. I have plenty of "toys" and a comfortable lifestyle: I own a home, have a car, take two or three vacations a year, and can buy tickets to sports, arts, and cultural events. To have these things and do these things, I have to operate within a budget, shop for sales, and, in some cases, make installment payments. But I consider what I do have and can do a blessing.

Even with everything I have going on in my life, it would be easy to focus on what I don't have. Advertising images online, in newspapers and magazines, on television and generated in your mind on radio constantly try to tempt you and me to buy the new thing on the market.

Unless you stop, look around and count your blessings, you could easily end up (like a laboratory rat) reacting to the flashing lights and sounds someone else makes to get you to do what *they* want you to do. You could get caught up in the hype of wanting "more" and buy more than you can afford. That's why I try to take time each day to be thankful for not only those *things* I have, but also for the good things that happen to me throughout the day. If I'm running late for a meeting and I find a parking place quickly, if I don't get a parking ticket, if someone unexpectedly says something that helps me solve a problem I say "Thank you, Lord."

I also try to remember what really counts: relationships with people. If you have family and/or one or two good friends—people you can count on, who have your best interest at heart, who have your back—you are truly blessed. Often times during news interviews people who lost everything in a hurricane, fire, tornado or flood are upset about the loss of their material possessions, but almost to a person say they are grateful they and their family are alive—that things can be replaced but people can't.

I'm grateful to be alive. The Greek philosopher Cicero once said, "Where there's life, there's hope." What that means to me is that as long as I'm vertical and breathing, things can get better. I'm grateful for my physical and mental health. I'm grateful to live in a country that—with all its flaws, shortcomings and challenges—has given me the freedom to choose my careers. I'm grateful that, because of those choices, my willingness to work hard, and the spirit to overcome obstacles that my parents gave me, I am in a position to help others. And I'm grateful because I have come to know (based on real life experiences) that there is a God who's got my back, even if no one else does.

By keeping all these things in mind I'm able to enjoy material things without becoming a slave to them, which helps create a nice balance in my life.

"NO" IS NOT A BAD WORD

"No" is part of the English language and you have every right to use it. Don't let people talk you into doing something you don't feel comfortable with.

People will sometimes try to make you feel badly about yourself by telling you you're not cool or you're stuck up or you think you're better than they are when you don't go along with *their* program. They may even say, "If you were *really* my friend" or "If you *really* loved me," you'd do what they want you to do.

Don't fall for that line. People who really care about you aren't going to try to get you to do something they know makes you uncomfortable.

When I was in college, some of my schoolmates smoked pot. I didn't. When the drugs came out at the party, I left. Doing drugs was not me. Also, I wasn't about to risk getting arrested or kicked out of school just to get people to like me. At first my actions made people uncomfortable. Some stopped inviting me to their parties, but others continued to invite me and let me know when the party was going in another direction so I could leave. They respected my choice to do what was right for me. I respected them for respecting me.

It's not easy saying no. Everyone likes to be liked. But you have to make decisions based on what's right for you—not on what will make you popular. Being popular is not always the road to the good life. It could be the road to decisions you later regret—decisions that keep you from achieving *your* definition of the good life.

So, don't be afraid to use "no" freely. If something doesn't feel right, don't do it, no matter who is trying to talk you into it. The very people who try to talk you into doing something many times won't be there for you when things go wrong.

Test yourself every morning. When you look in the mirror can you look yourself in the eye and feel good about the person you see? If not, you may be doing something you don't feel good about. Figure out what it is and stop it.

Make Time to Do Things You Enjoy

Everybody is busy doing something almost every minute of the day. Whether it's school, work, community service, church, or any number of other things that demand your time, there don't seem to be enough hours in the day to get everything done. In addition to our *To Do* list, the electronic devices we have make it virtually impossible to unplug and have time to think or relax.

Relaxation is important. In fact, it is essential. It allows you to recharge your batteries so you can think more clearly. It improves your outlook on life and helps you maintain a more positive mental attitude. Relaxation allows you to be more creative in whatever you do because it helps your mind remain open to viewing the world from different perspectives, and approaching situations you encounter in new ways.

That's why I treat fun time as seriously as I do work time. I make time to do things I enjoy. I love sports. I have a season ticket to the Milwaukee Bucks basketball games. I downhill ski with like-minded members of the Ebony Ice Ski Club. I love to travel. I make sure I take several trips each year to places I haven't been before so I can see and do things I can't see and do at home. I love to read. I belong to a book club. I love the arts. I have a membership to the Milwaukee Art Museum, and a season ticket to the Milwaukee Repertory Theatre. I attend performances by the Milwaukee Symphony, Hansberry-Sands Theatre Company and Ko-Thi Dance Company, as well as other arts and cultural events throughout the year. I belong to a group called

The Arts Group, whose members love and attend arts events. Being a member of this group gives me someone to go to arts events with. I love history and learning new things. I have a membership to the Milwaukee Public Museum.

Having these memberships and pursuing these interests not only keep me busy, but also provide me with a social network of people who share my interests. So, even though I am single and have no children, I have an extended family that supplements the relationship I have with my biological family. When I didn't show up for a book club meeting and forgot to call to say I wouldn't be there, one of the members called to make sure I was all right.

All work and no play is not healthy. Taking time for fun helps you lead a healthier, happier life.

WE ALL NEED SPACE

It's hard to find a place or time to just "be" these days. When I was in college I would sometimes go to a park, lay on my back and watch the clouds. Now it seems as if there's no time to do anything but work and do things that have to be done.

All of the technical devices in our lives have made things even more hectic. While it's true these devices make it easier for us to get things done, they also add to our *To Do* list. Cell phones keep us in constant contact, which means people can interrupt our plans for the day at any time. Email comes in faster than you can get through it. The waterfall of emails is largely due to robot search engines and "cookies" attached to websites we visit that put our email address on lists we never asked to be on. It's also due, in part, to people hitting the "Reply to All" button on matters that don't require a response to the whole group. Hundreds of broadcast channels mean you can spend your whole life doing nothing but watching television or listening to the radio. Entertainment options—sports, parties, movies, arts and cultural events, festivals, concerts, you name it—are nearly endless, and are always vying for your time.

We are surrounded by sound from televisions, radios, iPods, CD players, and traffic. Our eyes are assaulted by advertising messages on digital billboards and signs. In urban and suburban areas we are constantly around people—interacting with them nearly every hour of the day. We talk on the phone while walking, riding, driving. We're often thinking about what we have to do next. People with good causes are always asking for a little of our time to help out. All of these things that are vying for our attention are layered on top of family commitments we must take care of. It's hard to feel really at ease. The result is we rarely have quiet time to reflect on what's going on in our lives, what's important to us, what we really want from life, what difference we want to make in the world, and what we need to do to achieve our goals. Instead, we do one thing and then another without really thinking about it. Often we're so busy or feel so stressed we don't even think about the potential negative consequences of our actions on ourselves and others. Instead of taking time to think and make good decisions, we rush to get to the next thing on our "to do" list. In our haste to get things done, we run the risk of making decisions that can cost us our dreams.

I'm not knocking modern conveniences. I have a cell phone. I use email. There are broadcast channels I'm really glad exist because they carry programming I enjoy. I volunteer to help others. I certainly take advantage of a wide variety of entertainment opportunities. But it seems to me this constant state of motion, activity and doing may explain why people (increasingly) are short-tempered. I believe part of what it means to be human is to feel we have done things that truly matter to us, and that our presence on earth makes a difference. I believe frustration at not doing what matters to us (because of other time demands) and not making a difference frequently expresses itself in the form of anger.

We all need space to get to know ourselves—what we really want, feel, like, don't like, and believe in. We all need space to figure out why we are here on earth, and what we want our legacy to be—what we want to be remembered for. Finding that space in a fast-paced world isn't easy, but it's important to create a space for ourselves where we can find peace, think, and feel good about who we are. It may be a room, a chair, a place in the basement or attic, a closet, a place in a café, a place in the library, a place near a lake, a park bench. Wherever it is, we need to go there at least once a week (if not once a day) to get in tune with ourselves. I believe if each of us takes time to find our space, the peace it brings us will be reflected in the world around us.

Learn to Like Your Own Company

I've heard people say they can't stand being alone. They need to have people around them all the time. They need to be in the mix. They don't know what to do with themselves when they don't have someone to talk to or do things with.

I know human beings are social animals. It is part of our biology to want to be with others. But I've always wondered: if you don't want to be around yourself, why should anyone else want to be around you? Put another way, if you want other people to like being around you, you have to learn to like your own company.

One of the things that makes liking your own company possible is being an interesting person. You can do that by developing a wide range of interests that give you options for entertaining yourself. Having more interests increases your social options; the more things you like to do, the more people you have to do things with because each different activity has its own circle of people who share that interest.

Learning new things, trying new things, doing new things helps keep you from becoming bored. It also helps build self-esteem. Every time you successfully do something new you add to your list of accomplishments, which gives you greater confidence in your abilities. Being more confident makes you feel more comfortable in a wider variety of situations, which helps make you a more pleasant person to be around.

So to avoid being lonely and bored, expand your interests:

- Read books.
- Play a sport or go to sporting events.
- Go to a museum (art, science, history).
- Learn to dance, draw, paint, play an instrument, make your own clothes or jewelry, cook, fix a car.
- Get a hobby—something you like to do for the fun of it.
- Find something you like to collect (t-shirts, coins, cups, postcards, etc.).
- Plant a garden.
- Write.
- Join or form a singing group.
- Volunteer time to help someone.

The list of things to do will vary from person to person. But the reward for stretching yourself will be the same—you will enjoy your life whether you're entertaining yourself or hanging out with others.

BORED?

I've never understood how someone could say they're bored because "there's nothing to do." There are so many different people, places and things in the world that, even if I lived to be 1,000 years old, I couldn't see or do them all.

I believe you get bored if you limit your view of what life has to offer. The key to keeping things fresh is to open your eyes and your mind to what's going on around you, and to set goals for yourself so you will always have something to look forward to.

Those goals could be personal, professional, spiritual, physical, educational, or involve community service. If you give yourself the freedom to explore new *positive* opportunities, the list of interesting things to do is endless. In case you have trouble thinking of things to do, here's a *starter list*. When you have:

- Read every book ever written
- Read every newspaper in the world
- Read every magazine in the world
- Seen every play in the world
- Seen every work of art in the world
- Heard every piece of music ever created
- Danced every dance in the world
- Watched every movie ever made
- Visited every museum in the world
- Attended every sporting event in the world

- Played every sport in the world
- Eaten every food in the world
- Talked to every person in the world
- Visited every town, village, city, and unincorporated place on earth
- Climbed (literally) every mountain in the world
- Watched a sunrise and sunset from every place in the world
- Traveled by every mode of transportation in the world
- Traveled on every body of water in the world
- Visited every park in the world
- Seen every animal on the planet
- Seen every plant on earth
- Learned to speak every language on earth
- Attended every church in the world
- Helped every human being in need in the world . . .

Then you can be bored.

DEALING WITH PEOPLE

THERE'S A DIFFERENCE BETWEEN FRIENDS AND ACQUAINTANCES

The word friend is used all the time. People who have only known each other a short time will talk about someone being their friend. I believe there is a difference between friends and acquaintances.

Acquaintances are people you know. You may have known them for years, but your relationship with them is often casual and superficial. The longer you live, the more acquaintances you will have. You meet acquaintances in school, on your job, at church, at social outings. They may be nice. They may be fun to be around. But for them to qualify as friends takes more than a superficial relationship.

Friends are people who:

- Aren't hanging with you because they have an agenda—something they want from you. They are not your friend because of who you know or what you have. They are your friend because they like you, and care about you as much as they care about themselves. They have your best interest at heart.
- Work as hard at maintaining the friendship as you do. If you're doing all the work to maintain the relationship you have an acquaintance, not a friend.
- Like you for who you are. They are not constantly trying to make you over in the image of who *they* think you should be.
- Are honest with you about your good qualities *and* your shortcomings. We all love to have people tell us how wonderful

we are, how smart we are, how good looking we are. It's good for our self-confidence. Friends help boost your self-confidence. But we all have things about us we need to improve, and a friend will point out our flaws, especially when they are harmful to us or are keeping us from achieving something we really want in life. Sometimes friends will tell us gently about our flaws, but they are also willing to use tough love to help us turn away from something that will harm us. They won't let us fall into a pothole without letting us know the pothole is there.

- Will help you think through problems and come up with solutions that are good for you. They are willing to give you the unvarnished truth when you ask for their opinion or advice.
- You can depend on to be there for you in good times and bad. They have your back. They won't let anyone or anything blindside you. They're there to offer a shoulder to lean on. And they're there to laugh hard with you until your stomachs hurt.
- You can trust not to spread your business around to everybody else.
- Will not let disagreements or arguments destroy the friendship. Even when you have an argument, you will patch up the difference and still be friends.
- Are people of their word. If they say they're going to do something, you don't have to worry about it being done.
- Are happy for your successes, not jealous. They try to help you achieve your dreams rather than work to hold you back.

Being a friend is not easy. That's why most of us will have more acquaintances in life than real friends. But a good friend is worth his or her weight in gold. He or she is one of life's true blessings.

WHAT SOMEONE DOES IS MORE TRUE
THAN WHAT THEY SAY

I've learned that what someone does is a better indication of the truth than what they say. If someone says they're your friend but they talk about you behind your back, they're not your friend. If someone says they care about you but when you get sick they can't find time to check on you to see how you're doing or ask if there's anything you need, they don't really care about you.

People can and will tell you anything. They may lie about what they do for a living, whether they are married, whether they've ever been in jail, whether they are religiously devout, whether they have children, whether they are dating someone, whether they take drugs, how much education they have. You name it, people will lie about it. That's why it's important to spend time getting to know someone. Anyone can pretend to be something they're not for a while. But most people can't sustain their "act" for more than a year. Eventually they will fall back into old habits. If they're faking it, time will show you who they really are.

When most people lived in small towns it was easier to really know who a person was, what their values were, and whether or not they could be trusted. In fact, people often not only knew the individual but also other members of the family and, sometimes, the family history. If members of a family were known to steal, everyone knew it. If they were known to lie, everyone knew it.

Many of us now live in larger urban and suburban communities with people we may know by sight and may even speak to. But we don't have enough contact with them to really *know* them. People are more mobile. They may have been born in one place but moved to several other communities in their lifetime. Because of this mobility, they can invent a whole new image of themselves that has nothing to do with reality.

So whether you're deciding who you can share your personal thoughts and business with, or who you want to date or marry, or who to lend your favorite CD or iPod to—the wise thing to do is to be friendly but watchful. If you see someone doing things that contradict what they say, believe what they do, rather than what they say. If you're considering dating or marrying someone and you see some things about them you really don't feel comfortable with, don't make the mistake of thinking you can change them. No one can change someone who doesn't want to change. Instead, discuss your concerns and watch to see whether they make a change. If not, believe what you see. It will save you a lot of grief and disappointment.

TRUST YOUR INSTINCTS

It happens all the time. You'll meet someone, someone will say something to you, or you'll find yourself in a situation that sets off a little alarm inside of you. That alarm may be a thought, an uneasy feeling, a slight hesitation, a catch in the middle of your chest or the pit of your stomach, a tightening in the back of your neck, a hunch. Most times we ignore the feeling and move on. But, I've learned that little alarm is there for a reason. It's trying to tell you something you need to know for your own good. You should pay attention to it and try to figure out what's going on.

My parents and grandparents had a saying: "Follow your first mind." By that they meant your first reaction is most likely the correct one. Most times you'll end up doing the right thing.

I think a lot of times people get into trouble not because they are looking for trouble or problems, but because they ignore the warning sign—the little alarm—that goes off when they're facing a choice. If someone say's "let's go for a ride" and you know they only have a learner's permit, getting in the car with them could lead to trouble. If someone invites you to their home for a party and their parents are not there, that could lead to trouble. If someone asks you to hold or keep something for them and says "Don't tell anybody," that could lead to trouble.

The world is full of what I call sales people. They are trying to sell you on an idea, get you to go along with *their* program, convince you they've got the answer to whatever it is you're seeking an answer to, convince you they can resolve whatever issue you're dealing with. When I say "sales people," I'm not talking about sincere people who have your best interest at heart, and can actually help you. I'm talking about people who have a personal agenda that usually doesn't take into consideration the negative impact that going along with their program can have on *your* life.

When you encounter sales people and that little alarm goes off inside you, it is a signal you should be cautious. Stop and think about what you're about to do, and try to determine what's really going on before you jump on board. Don't just think about the benefits of doing something. Also think about what could go wrong. Decide whether the downside of taking an action will help or hurt your ability to achieve *your* life goals.

Paying attention to the little alarm that goes off inside you, and thinking about why you're hesitating can keep you out of a lot of trouble. It's easier to say "No" than to say "Yes" and have a mess to clean up.

No One Has the Right
to Make You Feel Bad

Some people seem to enjoy making other people feel bad. You know the type: you're feeling pretty good and they say something to put you down. They make fun of your dream when you tell them what you want to do in life, or they'll tell you why you can't achieve your dream. Before you know it you're feeling bad and, maybe, starting to doubt yourself.

I think people like that don't like themselves or the way their lives are going. They may have been hurt by someone or something that happened in their lives; or they may be jealous. Whatever the reason for their misery, they want others to feel as bad as they do.

Let me pause here and clarify something: I'm not saying you should not spend time with someone who is having a bad day. No matter how upbeat we are or try to be, we all have days when it's just not working for us. Sometimes we wake up in the morning and, for some reason, just can't get it together. Other times, things happen that turn a good day into a bad day: the death of a loved one; a disappointment connected with school, a job, a relationship; an illness or injury. At those times it's good to have others who can help us get through those hard times. But there is a difference between hanging around to help someone who is having a bad day and spending your time with someone who *continually* finds negative things to say, or who does things that make you feel bad about yourself.

There is no law that says you are required to stay around a person who is always pointing out the dark cloud in your sunny day, who does not treat you with respect, who tries to burst the bubble of your dreams, who tells you directly or through their actions that nobody likes you anyway, who tells you you can't do any better than you're doing now. *No one* has the *right* to make you feel bad. When you find yourself spending too much time with a human storm cloud, do what you can to help them get help but don't keep company with them indefinitely.

There's an old saying: "you can lead a horse to water but you can't *make* it drink"—meaning you can't force people to do something they are determined not to do. If you get sucked into someone else's depression there is the real danger that, instead of you pulling them up, their negativity will bring you down. If they want to remain miserable, nothing you do will cheer them up. *They* have to make the decision to change or seek/accept help to change their attitude. If they are deeply depressed, you can try to help them find professional help. But ultimately the decision to change is theirs to make.

Don't allow yourself to get trapped in *their* sinkhole. You were put on earth for a greater purpose than that.

LOVE IS NOT A PASS/FAIL TEST

When you hear the words, "If you really loved me you'd . . . (fill in the blank)," know this: these words are not about love. They are about getting you to go along with someone else's agenda. Love is *not* a pass/fail test. You don't have to "prove" your love to anyone.

1 Corinthians 13:4-8 probably said it best: "Love is patient and kind; it is not jealous or conceited or proud; love is not ill-mannered or selfish or irritable, love does not keep a record of wrongs; love is not happy with evil, but is happy with the truth. Love never gives up; and its faith, hope, and patience never fail. Love is eternal."

This is real love. Anything short of this is counterfeit.

Every Good-bye Ain't Gone

Things happen when there're supposed to, not necessarily on our time schedule. That's a hard lesson to learn and live with—especially in today's world where we've been conditioned to want things quick, fast and in a hurry. When something we want seems impossible or we "lose" it, that doesn't necessarily mean we're not supposed to have it. Instead it may mean it's just not our time in life to have it. We may need to mature more before we can handle and appreciate it.

The third chapter in the book of Ecclesiastes says "for everything there is a season and a time for every purpose under heaven . . ." Waiting for that season to come requires patience. Being patient is hard—especially when it comes to relationships. What you want may not be what you need at that point in your life—even if *you* think you do.

Building a lasting, loving relationship takes time. You have to get to know the person—the good, the bad and the ugly—so you can decide whether you can deal with *their* bad and ugly (and they can decide whether they can deal with *your* bad and ugly).

In many ways building a lasting, loving relationship is like building a friendship. Just because you know and like a person doesn't mean they're your friend. Friends are people you know will be there for you no matter what. Even when you have serious disagreements, the bond between friends is so strong that arguments cannot destroy the friendship. Friends care about each other and support each other's dreams; but they will also be honest and tell you the truth when they see you doing something that could cause you harm. Friends allow you to be yourself, but will also tell you about things that can help you become the person *you* say you want to be.

Sometimes you'll be attracted to someone who you're convinced is "the one," but things just don't go the way you want them to. It could be he or she isn't "the one." Or it could be your season together has not come. Only time will tell. That's where patience comes in.

If you've ever seen a child chasing a butterfly, you know nine times out of ten he or she never catches it. But when the child sits down and is quiet, often times the butterfly will come and land on him or her. It's the same with a relationship. Trying to force something to happen is usually futile—it either doesn't work out or you get what you want and regret it. It is better to wait for the right season. If it's meant to be, it will happen.

Even if it looks like things are not going to work out, they might. Every good-bye ain't gone. When the time is right, things work out for the best. In the meantime, enjoy the life you have and trust God to act in your best interest in due season. That certainly is a lot easier said than done, but the older you get the more you realize God doesn't make mistakes. You may not get everything you *think* you want in life, but what you do get will be in your best interest. Your patience will pay off.

PEOPLE WILL NOT ALWAYS BE FAIR

I am part of what I call the integration generation—the first large group of African Americans who entered grade school following the U.S. Supreme Court's *Brown vs Topeka Board of Education* decision, which ruled that segregated schools were not constitutional. Our generation's role was to walk through doors that, in the past, had been closed to African Americans. We were supposed to do our best academically and behave like ladies and gentlemen so that other African Americans coming up behind us would also have a chance to get a good education and be treated like full citizens with equal rights and opportunities.

Being a pioneer—even in the north—was not easy. Laws do not necessarily change people's hearts and minds. Sometimes people were just out and out mean—calling me names, looking at me in a way that let me know I wasn't wanted there, tripping me on the playground, intentionally bumping me in the hallway, throwing a baseball bat at my head. Sometimes even people who meant well could do harm, such as the high school guidance counselor who told me to take orchestra instead of German because I "needed the culture" (even though I really *needed* a foreign language to get into college, and was planning to major in psychology—a field dominated by German-speaking Sigmund Freud).

Another part of being a pioneer, I learned in school, was that if I wanted to get the same recognition as someone else I would have to work harder. In my high school physics class, my lab partner (a certified genius) and I got the same test grades and the same lab grades. The truth is, I was better in physics than he was. In lab, I helped him understand how to do the experiments. But, in the first marking period he got an A and I got a B. I asked my teacher what I had to do to get an A in the class, and he told me I had to do extra credit work. I did that extra work and got my A. It wasn't fair. But, as my parents told me, any extra knowledge I put in my brain was something nobody could take away from me. Doing extra work, I believed, made me more knowledgeable in physics than anyone in the class (other than the teacher). Having this attitude added to my self-confidence.

When I moved into the work world, I ended up training two of my bosses before I was promoted to manager. One of those I trained hadn't finished college. I had two college degrees: a bachelor's and a master's degree. Again, I didn't get mad about the unfairness of the situation. I made sure I did my job so well that the next time a promotion opportunity came up I couldn't be denied the position without raising embarrassing questions from senior management. I also learned to document my work in writing so I could "prove" my case for promotion if necessary. I got my promotion.

As much as I would like to say things like this don't happen any more, it's not true. But, while unfairness is *not* o.k., I decided long ago not to let it be a barrier to achieving what I want to in life. My focus is on what I want to do and what it will take to get there. My reward? When I achieve something others were trying to keep me from doing, it drives them nuts. It's fun to see the "How'd she do that?" look they get on their faces because they thought they had me boxed in . . . but they didn't. People will not always be fair. But they can't stop you from succeeding in life unless you let them.

Of course if the unfairness is a violation of the law, company policy, or other rules and regulations, follow the established process for challenging the unfairness.

Document the situation in writing. File a formal complaint. If the situation is bad enough, take legal action.

Having said this, don't spend your life challenging the routine day-to-day unfairness. All this will do is suck up time you could better spend on achieving *your* goals. Instead, develop a plan for getting over, under, around or through the barriers people put up in your life. Succeed despite your adversary's best efforts to stop you. It will drive them nuts.

Negative People Will Suck You Dry

I believe there are two basic types of people in the world—negative people and positive people.

Negative people are those who usually see the glass as half empty—meaning they see obstacles in life and don't believe there is a way to get around them. Because they can't see their way around obstacles, they don't believe things can get better. They don't think there is anything they can do to make things work out, and believe whatever happens in their life is out of their control. Even if someone tries to help them they either won't accept help, or they do something that makes the help not work.

When things don't work out, negative people frequently blame their problems on outside forces in their lives or on other people. They give in to hopelessness and, because of this, frequently are angry and, too often, end up being road kill—run over and flattened by circumstances. Often, because they feel bad about the way their life is going, they try to make those around them feel bad about *their* lives. Instead of encouraging someone, they are quick to tell another person why some idea they have won't work, or say a dream the person has is stupid, or say "they" won't let you do that. Their "humor" is often put-down humor. In the name of humor, they may ridicule how you talk or how you look or how you dress or the things you like to do.

Positive people, on the other hand, see the glass as half full. Yes, they see the obstacles. But they believe there is a way to get around them. They think about ways to get things done. They are willing to accept help, and are also willing to keep trying even if help doesn't come. They don't look for people or outside forces to blame when things don't go right. They look for solutions to *make* things right. Instead of doing the same thing over and over and getting the same results, they are not afraid to try something different. They have discipline—they will put in the time and effort it takes to achieve their goal. And, they have hope and believe that things can (and will) get better.

I try to surround myself with positive people. I don't mean I avoid someone because he or she is having a bad day or even a bad week or bad month or two. We all do. We all need people who aren't in the middle of what we're going through to help us see what is happening so we can get back on track. Nor am I talking about true friends who will point out dangers, threats or problems with things we're doing in life. Everyone needs someone who can help them think through major decisions and warn them when they see danger. What I'm talking about is the person I call the Dream Killer, who can rarely find anything positive to say about anything or anyone.

People who constantly view life negatively have a mental mindset that I'm not trained to help them get out of. I will give it a good, serious effort—usually measured in months. But if they insist on staying down in the valley, then it's time to help them find someplace where they can get help. This may be a parent, aunt or uncle, pastor, boss or professional counselor. If they don't want to do that, it's time to move on. I don't abandon them totally; I just don't hang out with them on a regular basis. I've learned through experience that spending a lot of time around negative people can sap your energy and wear you down. It's like trying to walk around wearing a fifty-pound backpack. It may not bother you at first, but eventually it will tire you out.

If you stay around them too long, negative people will suck you dry. Instead of you bringing them up, they will bring you down. Instead of you fulfilling the positive purpose you were put on earth to achieve, you'll likely end up taking your talent to the grave. We can't help everyone who comes into our lives. We can try to do the best we can. But it is important to recognize when it's time to place their situation in God's hands.

HATE AND ANGER WILL EAT YOU UP

There seem to be a lot of people walking around with that "Don't mess with me" look in their eyes. If you accidentally bump into them, they look at you like they want to knock your head off. Road rage—ranging from people gesturing and yelling like a maniac at another driver to something much more serious—is not uncommon. Minor disagreements escalate into arguments and fights. On more than one occasion I've read news stories about people joking around or mock-fighting one minute and then getting into a real fight where someone is shot or stabbed or killed because one person lost their temper over something the other person said or did. After the trial is over, the defendant (usually, but not always, male) says he's sorry and didn't mean to do it.

Why didn't a bell go off in his head and stop him *before* he hurt or killed someone? I think a big part of the answer to this uncontrolled anger and hate is not being able to forgive. Our society emphasizes individualism—every man and woman for themselves. The result is that some people are so focused on doing what works for *them* that they frequently don't think about the impact their actions have on others. As a result, they can rub people the wrong way without knowing it. The constant bombardment of insults and hurts dished out by people who are only thinking about themselves is like death by a thousand cuts. It creates wounds that, individually, only bleed a little; but collectively can bleed you dry emotionally. Eventually anger or hatred caused by these insults and hurts builds up and people blow up. The person that gets hurt when the blow-up happens may not even be the one responsible for causing the anger.

While I am not in any way justifying the blow-up, the reality is that there are things and people who will make you want to scream. The key is not to allow those things or those people to dominate your existence. Everything will not go exactly the way you want it to in life. You can't control everything that happens. What you *can* control is how you react to what happens. You can choose to let someone else pull your strings and keep you in a constant state of agitation, or you can choose to run your own life. You can choose to spend your time getting back at someone or spend it working toward achieving your dreams. You can choose to focus on the negative situation or you can choose to focus on those things that bring you joy. You can choose to focus on "Why me" or you can learn from what happened to reduce the likelihood it will happen again.

Controlling how you respond to life's challenges is not easy. You have to constantly work at it. But the benefits are worth it. Not only will it keep you out of trouble, but it will also help you realize your life goals. The time you spend plotting how to get back at someone is time you could spend working to achieve your dreams. If you lash out at someone, you could end up in legal trouble that derails your plans. Hate and anger can damage your health by creating stress. Scientist have proven getting angry on a regular basis, or constantly replaying old hurts in your mind can hurt your body's ability to combat illness. If this stress persists unchecked, it could shorten your life.

Hate and anger reduce the quality of your life physically as well as emotionally, so don't let these feelings dominate your life. Take control of how you respond to people who do things you don't like. In all likelihood, the person you're so angry with has gone on with their life, and you're the only one who's upset. Don't hurt yourself by hanging on to old grievances. Don't let hate and anger eat you up. Instead, focus on making the most out of your life, and making the world a better place because you were here.

IT TAKES TWO TO ARGUE

It takes two to argue. Even when you see a person walking down the street by themselves carrying on an angry conversation, he or she is arguing with someone in their head.

When I find myself in a situation where someone is trying to pick a fight or start an argument, instead of yelling back at them, I speak quietly. The louder they get the softer my voice gets. In most cases their volume will also come down. If that doesn't work, I walk away. I know that goes against the trend, which is to say outrageous things, yell, and argue; but I think that trend is why violence is growing in this country—from road rage to homicides. Yelling at each other doesn't solve the problem. It only makes the problem worse. People become more emotional, and then it's on.

Problems get solved when people can calmly explain to each other what the issue is and work toward a solution. Even if they agree to disagree, that is a solution. Reaching a solution makes a lot more sense to me then letting things escalate to the point where someone gets hurt physically or emotionally, because such hurts usually makes people want revenge. Plotting revenge sucks up time you could use working on fulfilling your dreams.

So don't let disagreements escalate into arguments. Instead, try working things out in a calm way. You'll appreciate that approach once you cool down.

TROUBLE CAN'T CATCH YOU
IF YOU WALK AWAY

Trouble can come into your life in many ways:

- Conflict: People who try to pick a fight with you, or try to make you react to what they're doing in a negative way, which can get you in trouble.

- Temptation: People who try to get you to do something you know is wrong. Your gut tells you to think about it, or you know it can lead to trouble because you've seen what it's done to other people.

- Bad company: Hanging around people who are always getting into trouble or trying to stir up trouble.

- Negative people: Spending time with people who try to make you stop believing in yourself and your dreams by constantly telling you what you can't do, or making fun of you because you're not acting the way *they* think you should act.

- Greed: Focusing on acquiring material things, and being willing to do anything—no matter who it hurts—to get them.

- Selfishness: Not caring about anybody but yourself.

- Shortcuts: Looking for the easy way to get something—or to get out of something—rather than the *right* way.

You can't stop all trouble from coming into your life; but you can decrease the likelihood that it will get a tight grip on you by paying attention to what's going on and walking *away* from trouble *toward* something more positive and productive that can help you achieve your dreams.

THE GOLDEN RULE IS NOT OLD SCHOOL

I believe a lot of the anger, hostility and violence that seems to be part of everyday life would go away if people would live by the Golden Rule—do unto others as you would have them do unto you. Instead of following this rule, people seem to be so focused on what they want that they act like they're the center of the universe, and the only thing that matters is what *they* want. This does not leave room for other people to have their needs and wants met.

Unless someone has issues that require professional help, most people don't consciously look for ways to hurt themselves or to make themselves unhappy. So, I believe if more people acted as though what they did or said to someone else would have a direct impact on them, they would be more careful about the things they do and say. It isn't hard:

- If you don't want someone treating you in a disrespectful manner, don't treat them in a disrespectful manner.
- If you don't want someone yelling at you, don't yell at them.
- If you don't want somebody calling you a name that hurts your feelings, don't call someone else a name that hurts their feelings.
- If you don't want someone talking about you behind your back, don't talk about someone else behind their back.
- If you don't want someone to publicly embarrass or humiliate you, don't publicly embarrass or humiliate them.

- If you don't want someone to bully you, don't bully them.
- If you don't want someone cutting you off in traffic, don't cut them off in traffic.
- If you don't want someone to make you feel you can't achieve your dreams, don't do or say things to make someone else feel they can't achieve their dreams.

Frederick Douglass, the former slave and eloquent 19th Century anti-slavery crusader once said, "Where justice is denied, where poverty is enforced, where ignorance prevails, and where any one class is made to feel that society is an organized conspiracy to oppress, rob and degrade them, neither persons nor property will be safe."

While he was speaking specifically about the inequality created by the institution of slavery, his remarks ring true for any situation in which people feel they are being treated unfairly. When people feel they have been harmed in some way, they may focus on "getting back." Resentment leads to anger, which can build up. They snap. You snap. And the next thing you know something happens that everyone regrets—someone gets seriously hurt, killed, or—in the case of bullying—the person who is bullied sometimes commits suicide. All the regret in the world can't bring a dead person back to life, or undo the physical or emotional injury inflicted on another person.

If we really want peace and calm to exist in our homes, on our block, in our community and in our world, we have to make the Golden Rule a part of our daily lives. The Golden Rule is *not* old school.

KINDNESS IS NOT A WEAKNESS

Acting tough seems to be the accepted norm among some individuals. Those who are nice are considered "soft."

I think this attitude contributes to much of the growing violence that occurs not just in urban centers, but also in suburbs and small towns. People seem to get angry and snap more quickly—often over things that, in hindsight, were fairly trivial.

Kindness wasn't considered a weakness when I was growing up. Instead it was a way of life, and helped create a positive environment in which to grow up and live. Several childhood memories illustrate this point:

- All adults took on the parent role and looked out for all children. Mrs. Hattie Fountain, who lived down the street from my house, was not related to me. I played with her grandchildren. When I mentioned one day that I liked her piano, she asked whether I would like to take lessons. I told her yes. She asked me to bring her my report card to see whether I was doing well in school. I was. My parents paid for the piano lessons that I took on Mrs. Fountain's piano until they could buy a piano. It was the start of my love for music. Another example of all adults being parents occurred when I was old enough to be left at home with my brother. My parents went out for the evening. They told me if I got scared or needed anything, I should go to Mr. and Mrs. McCoy's house. A thunderstorm came up. The noise frightened me. I took my brother, Renato, up to the McCoy's, where they gave us milk and cookies and put us to bed. When my parents came home and saw we weren't there, they came to the McCoys' house to pick us up and take us home.

- If you made eye contact with another person, whether you knew them or not, you smiled and spoke. That was the Southern tradition. If, as a child, you didn't speak—especially to an adult—your parent would say, "Girl (boy), don't you know how to speak!?"
- People would sit on the front porch and talk with each other on hot summer days.
- If a child got out of hand, a parent would go talk over the situation with the other parent and get the matter resolved without arguing or fighting.
- Children were expected to work things out rather than fight. When fights did occur, adults worked together to straighten out the problem so it wouldn't happen again.
- When the block I lived on started experiencing problems, the adults formed a block club to make sure the city picked up the garbage the way they were supposed to, the police came when called, and properties were properly maintained—even by absentee landlords.

The focus when I was growing up was on community—working together for the good of all concerned. You were expected to be polite and treat others with respect. People didn't have to "demand" respect—it was automatically given. Caring about each other was not considered a sign of weakness, but a sign of "good home training." The result: we didn't have many fights break out among young people. We didn't have nearly the level of crime and violence we have now. No one had ever heard of "road rage." You didn't have to have deadbolt locks on your door.

I believe if we went back to this way of dealing with each other, we could change communities for the better. Once you get past the necessities—food, clothing and shelter—what most human beings want is to be treated with respect, kindness and caring. It doesn't cost anything to treat people with kindness; and the return on that investment can go a long way toward creating peace and harmony in our communities, our schools, our work places and our world.

PLEASE AND THANK YOU

There are three words in the English language that can change how people interact with you—"please" and "thank you."

It sounds too simple to be true. But it is. Having grown up in a time when saying those words was just what you did, I noticed that when I use them today I get a positive response from people who, when I first started interacting with them, might not have been as pleasant. A clerk at a store who has just rung me up and never looked at me, will look at me and smile when I use those words. A young man wearing the obligatory smile-free face while holding a door open for me will stand up a little taller when I say "Thank you." A customer service representative who may not be especially helpful will change his or her tone of voice when I use those words.

Everyone likes to be appreciated. Everyone likes to be treated with respect. Saying please and thank you is an easy way to show that you appreciate and respect someone, and recognize that they are a human being just like you.

Try it. You'll notice the change it makes in your day-to-day dealings with people.

You Can Be Tough-Minded Without Being Hard-hearted

I have always had a tendency to be a people pleaser. I want others to be happy. But I've learned over the years that not everyone has respect for that trait. There are those who will latch on like leeches and try to freeload their way through life at your expense. Sometimes they'll play the sympathy card, telling you a sad story. Sometimes they'll pretend to be your friend. Sometimes they'll ask for a "one-time" favor and then show up again and again. The fact of the matter is they are out for themselves, and will hang around for as long as you let them.

Now, I believe in helping others and will go out of my way to do so, but I've learned not to "help" them indefinitely. I've learned the difference between those asking for help who are really trying to get back on their feet and those asking for help because they don't want to take the initiative to stand on their own two feet.

If it's a non-emergency situation, I will ask questions to find out what someone needs, what they have done to help themselves, and who else in their lives might be able to help them. In non-emergency situations, I will make suggestions about where they can get help (based on what I know is available and works). If I can't make a direct referral, I will try to find out who might be able to help them, and share that information. The ones who are really seeking help to get back on their feet will follow up on this information. The ones who want a free ride are likely to be what I call "yeah but" people. They will always be able to tell you why every suggestion you make won't or didn't work (even though you know the referral place has helped others in similar situations).

If I feel someone is trying to play me stupid, I cut them loose no matter how long they've known me. I do this not because I'm hard-hearted, but because I've come to recognize that I can't do it all. There are plenty of people out there who really need and want a hand up. I would rather spend my time doing things that actually help people move on with their lives than carry a freeloader on my back.

People May Not Like You, But You Can Earn Their Respect

For any number of reasons, everybody is not going to like you. The most common reasons for someone not liking you are:

- They just don't feel a connection with you.
- Someone said something about you (whether it's true or false).
- Jealousy.
- They don't feel comfortable around you because:
  - The way you carry yourself leads them to have an opinion about you that may or may not be true.
  - They have issues related to their own sense of self-worth.

You're not going to change someone's mind (no matter what you do) if they are determined not to like you. So, as my mother would say, "Don't try to buy your friendship." Don't twist yourself into a pretzel and dedicate your life to trying to make someone your friend. If they don't want to be bothered with you, leave them alone.

While you can't make everyone like you, you can earn people's respect:

- **Show your respect for others by treating them the way you want to be treated.** This includes being polite and considerate.

- **Be fair.** Even if someone doesn't agree with you, if they feel you are being fair in your dealings with them, they will respect you for it.

- **Be a person of your word.** If you say you're going to do something, do it. If you can't, let someone know in time for them to make other plans. Being known as someone who's dependable is a major plus in life. It will open doors for you. Sometimes even those who don't like you will open doors to opportunities or, at least, not try to block your way because they know you will get things done, and done right.

- **Be honest.** Don't mislead someone. If you accidentally do, apologize and let them know what happened. People appreciate others who are straight with them.

- **Be yourself.** People can sense when you're a phony, and they often resent that.

- **Carry yourself with dignity.** By that I don't mean walking around like you're better than anybody else. I mean walking around like you have the right to be treated with respect just like anyone else (because you do).

- **Be aware of the message you're sending about yourself by the way you dress, the way you talk, and the language you use.** People pick up clues about the type of person you are based on these things.

- **Be aware of the message you're sending about yourself based on the people you hang out with.** People assume "birds of a feather flock together." This is not about thinking you're better than someone else; it's about the message you send to others about who you are and how you want to be treated (based on the company you keep).

Ultimately, I think, respect has more value than being liked because it's something we all seem to crave as human beings. Arguments, fights, wars, and acts of violence often come down to one thing—someone feeling disrespected. Earning and giving respect can help reduce the likelihood that hostilities will break out.

OVERCOMING CHALLENGES

Nobody Owes You a Free Ride in Life

Some people seem to have an entitlement mentality: they act as if the world owes them something simply because they're here. When things don't go their way, they complain. When they hit obstacles in life—which happens to everyone—they expect someone to take care of the situation for them. They don't look for ways around life's obstacles, but rather blame others when they can't get what they want. In their minds they are never at fault for anything that goes wrong in their lives.

Those who go through life expecting others to give them whatever they want or need will be very disappointed. Certainly people are willing to help during emergencies and disasters, but most are not willing to make helping the same person over and over again their life's work. They get tired of helping the same individuals or groups after a while, and may even start questioning why their help is still needed even when it's obvious the need still exists. Within the social service field, this is known as "compassion fatigue."

At any point, any one of us could find ourselves in need. At those times there is no shame in asking for and accepting help. But depending on others to be there on a *regular* basis is like walking on thin ice in late spring—there's a good chance you'll fall through the cracks. The truth is, no one owes anyone a free ride. So, it does not make sense to look for one. What does make sense is to be prepared to live by an old saying from down South: "The best place to find a helping hand is at the end of your own arm." If you get outside help on top of that, that's a bonus.

Nothing Good Comes Easy

It would be nice if all you had to do is say you wanted something to happen and it happened, or say you wanted something and you got it. Unfortunately, that's not how life works. The reality is that nothing good comes easy. You're not going to get the big corner office with the great view making big money without the education to get your foot in the door in the first place. No matter what field you go into—plumbing, education, business, carpentry, medicine, law, sports, entertainment, politics, science, engineering, music, whatever—you're not going to start your career at the top. You have to work your way up.

You wouldn't know that by watching television or movies or reading lifestyle magazines. For the most part they focus on the results without showing what it takes to get those results. You see the bling but rarely hear the back story about how much time and effort it took to get to that point: how much education was required, how much planning it took, how much practice it took, how many work hours were put in each week, or how much continuing education and training is needed to stay competitive. To live a moderately comfortable middle income life—where you know you can eat regularly, wear clothes, live indoors, take vacations, buy and maintain a home and car, do *some* of the things you like to do for fun, and have something left over for retirement—takes a lot of time and effort. The reality for most of us is that it will take most of a lifetime to get where we want to be in life. In other words, it takes not only effort, but patience (understanding that we're not going to get everything we want right now this minute), and perseverance (hanging in there when things get tough, and thinking our way over, under or around situations and people that stand between us and what we are trying to achieve).

Effort, patience and perseverance aren't just important for getting "stuff." They're even more important for building lasting relationships in life. As social animals, most of us like spending time around other people at least some time during the day; and most of us want to have close relationships with people we can have fun with and depend on. Maintaining true friendships—the type that last through thick and thin, agreements and disagreements, good days and bad—doesn't just happen. It takes work. True friends look out for each other's well being, which means sometimes one friend may have to sacrifice doing something he or she wants to do to help the other friend. The same is true in marriage. Maintaining a good marriage requires a mutual commitment to caring about the well-being of the other person.

Whether it's about achieving a comfortable lifestyle or maintaining personal relationships, anything worth having takes work. Or, as Benjamin Franklin once said "There are no gains without pains."

GOOD TIMES AND BAD TIMES
DON'T LAST FOREVER

The Greek philosopher Heraclitus once said that the only constant in life is change. From one day to the next—sometimes one moment to the next—things can and do change. Your day may be going well, and then something happens to make things fall apart. On the other hand, things could be going badly and then something happens to make circumstances improve. The key to dealing with this reality is to recognize it for what it is—a temporary situation—and continue to move forward.

I know this is easier said than done, especially if the "bad" thing catches you off guard. Unless it's a life-threatening situation, the best thing to do when something goes wrong is to pause, catch your breath, and step back mentally to assess where things are. Depending on how serious the situation is, you might also want to think about who can help you, or whose good judgment you respect enough to bounce ideas off of. (By good judgment I mean someone who, on a regular basis, is able to get past problems and get their life back on track. You don't want to take advice from someone who is always in trouble, or always seems to be in crisis.) Once you've thought things through and received good advice, put together a plan of action and take steps to get your life back on track.

Patience is required when things go wrong. This also is easier said than done because we live in a fast-paced world where we've come to expect quick results. But snap decisions in non-life-threatening situations often make matters worse rather than better, and can also make putting things back in order even harder to do.

Recognizing that a bad situation is temporary can help keep your spirits up and your mind clear so you can find a way out. If you become too focused on *The Problem* you may not see an obvious solution right there in front of you. On the other side of the coin, expecting good times to last forever is setting yourself up for disappointment. It could also throw you into a tailspin, making you feel worse than you otherwise would. Life is not perfect. You cannot control everything that happens. Expecting things to be good all the time is not realistic.

It takes a lot of practice to get to the point where you can deal with life changes in a way that doesn't knock you off your feet. But by keeping things in perspective (for example, remembering past situations where things worked out for the best, and past successes in overcoming problems) your highs won't be too high and your lows won't be too low for you to get your life back in balance when change (inevitably) comes.

COMPLAINING IS JUST THE FIRST STEP

Complaining doesn't change anything. Sure, it's natural to complain when something isn't going the way you want it to. We all complain. But the only way to make things better is to take action.

Think about it. If you slip and fall into a mud puddle, complaining about it won't help you get back on your feet. The only way you'll get out of the puddle is to push yourself up or have someone help you up. It's the same when you face problems in life. Talking about them over and over won't make problems go away. You have to deal with them by:

- Thinking about what it will take to change your situation.
- Putting together a plan to take you from where you are to where you want to be.
- Implementing the plan—that is, taking the steps necessary to make change happen.

I found myself in a work situation that was so stressful I ended up in the emergency room throwing up and having chest pains. At first the doctors thought I was having a heart attack. They found out it was a stress attack brought on by problems I was having with some of my co-workers. I was only in my 30s, too young to have these health issues. I decided I wanted to leave the job. But the job market wasn't that great, and I still had a long way to go before I could retire, so I couldn't just quit.

I thought about what I wanted to do and remembered I had written in my high school yearbook that I wanted to own my own newspaper. That idea didn't seem feasible, but the idea of going into business for myself caught my attention. My thinking was that working for myself meant I wouldn't have to deal with co-workers who were constantly trying to undercut me. I started talking to people who owned their own businesses to gather as much information as possible about what it would take to be successful. I took advantage of business and management classes offered through my company. I read newspaper and magazine articles and books about successful business owners, and watched business programs on public television.

I took an inventory of myself, figuring out what my needs were and, more importantly, what my fears were about being totally responsible for earning every dime I made. That led me to pay off my bills, buy and stock a deep freezer with food, and stockpile canned foods. By doing this I felt certain I wouldn't starve to death or have to worry about paying for a place to stay.

Finally, I bought the equipment and supplies I needed for my business while I was still working, and started working on my own time to build up a client base.

All of this took about four years. I was thinking about leaving at that time, but found out if I stayed one more year the company would owe me a pension when I retired. So I stayed on the job another year.

What kept me sane for those five years were two things:

- I turned the "crazy" people who were getting on my last nerve over to God and let Him handle them. One by one they either left the company or left the department where I worked.
- I kept my mind focused on my goal—to build up my business and leave the company. Focusing on the solution (what I needed to do to leave the company) rather than the problem helped me stay healthy and reasonably happy. I knew whatever insanity I might have to deal with was temporary.

You can nudge life in the direction you want it to go by focusing on your goals. Yes, you identify the problem. That's necessary. But then you start looking at what your options are for dealing with that problem. To determine your options, you need to do some homework. Read books and articles on others who have successfully overcome problems (if possible, similar problems). Seek out and talk with knowledgeable people (in my case, someone who was running a successful business).

Then pick the options that seem most likely to get you past your problem. Start working on the solution, and make whatever adjustments in your plan and your actions you need to along the way. Taking this approach will help you in several ways:

- You won't get stuck in the mud of life.
- You will become more knowledgeable, which will help you become more skilled at assessing situations, making good decisions, and avoiding pitfalls.
- You will gain more confidence in yourself and your ability to overcome whatever curve balls life throws at you. As a result, you'll be more likely to achieve many of your life goals.

A Setback is a Knockdown, Not a Knockout

Life is not a straight line from point A to point Z. Instead, it zigzags: one step forward, two steps back; two steps forward one step back, four steps forward three steps back.

Even when you think things through, identify your goals, put together a game plan for reaching those goals, and stick to your plan, you're bound to run into situations that throw you back on your heels. When this happens it can be discouraging. Don't give up. A setback is a knockdown *not* a knockout . . . unless you stay down.

To get back on your feet and start moving forward again, take time to look at where things are. Is this a minor glitch or a major problem? Is this something you can handle on your own, or will you need help? If you need help, who can provide it? Is there a way to get help for free or at a low cost? If not, what will it cost to get help, and how can you legally get the money to pay for it? For example, can you make installment payments? What caused the setback, and what can you do in the future to prevent it from happening again? What do you need to do to get things back on track?

Estimate how long it will take you to get back on track, and put together a written timeline or calendar for getting things done. What temporary and permanent changes will you need to make in the way you spend your time in order to get your life back on track?

Sometimes what you *think* is a setback is not really a setback, but rather a new door opening to opportunities you might not have considered before. Make sure you look at what happens not only in terms of how it derails your plans, but also in terms of whether it offers opportunities that are better than your original goal.

My career plan had always been to work as a newspaper reporter. About five years into the job, I decided I wanted to become an editor. Those opportunities did not seem available where I was working, so I decided to leave that job and go work for another paper. I was an award-winning journalist. I was working for one of the top 10 newspapers in the country. I figured getting another newspaper job would be easy.

It wasn't.

I interviewed at a number of publications and did not get a single offer (even though I had won a state press club award for a series I co-wrote). Discouraged, I went to a job fair in town and handed out my resume to anyone who would take it—including the Army and the Navy. One of the companies at the job fair was Miller Brewing Company. They had an opening in their public relations department. Back in those days a news person who took a job in public relations was thought to be making a move to the "dark side." I felt like Darth Vadar from Star Wars: a Jedi Knight who had joined the forces of evil. But I took the job with the hope that the broader experience I would get working for Miller would make me more marketable as an editor. It didn't work out that way, but the *setback* turned out to be a positive career move. Not only did I make more money, but I also acquired skills that allowed me to start my own business. That led to other career moves that, eventually, allowed me to retire early and start focusing on doing the thing I enjoy most—writing.

My "setback" became the setup for a major step up.

DON'T LET FEAR AND DOUBT
TAKE YOU OUT

Two of the most potent enemies of success are internal, not external. Too often people don't achieve their life-long dreams because of *fear* and *doubt*.

The most common fear is *fear of trying something new*. Even though opportunity may be staring them in the face, too often people are afraid to reach out and take advantage of an opportunity because it requires them to do something they've never done before. Trying something new certainly is scary—especially if it's something no one you know personally has done. But, as my parents told me when I was growing up, if another human being is capable of achieving something, I can too. All I have to do is get the education and skills I need, be willing to work hard, believe in myself, and give my best effort. Following their instructions, I've gained skills and had opportunities to do things I could not have imagined as a young person:

- Although I was shy, I majored in journalism in college (a job that requires you to talk to strangers), and became an award-winning reporter for one of the top newspapers in the country.
- My next job was in the male-dominated beer business, where I became an award-winning public relations manager for two of the company's brands. That job gave me opportunities to work with company executives, and travel (on occasion) on the company plane, and in limos.

- Even though my marketing business was so small I ran it out of my home, I was chosen to be a delegate to the White House Conference on Small Business.
- I was the first female and first African American to chair a policy-making body for the waste water treatment agency that serves four southeastern Wisconsin counties. During my tenure, the board oversaw a $2.1 billion sewer construction project. As part of my job, I interacted with and was involved in tough negotiations with government officials regarding payment for the project. I also occasionally had meetings with some of the area's business leaders.
- I wrote the libretto (lyrics) for an opera.
- Although I had no previous television experience, I became a freelance producer for my local public television station by building on the skills I had developed as a newspaper reporter.
- I learned how to invest money, which allowed me to retire early.

Along the way there were many people who questioned whether I could do any of these things. A few times I had doubts, also. Had I not overcome my fear and doubt, my life would have been much less productive and fulfilling. But, I remembered what my parents said, and I remembered the words from 2 Timothy 1:7—"For God has not given us a spirit of fear and timidity, but of power, love, and self-discipline."

When you are faced with fear and doubt, remember these words. Don't let these two enemies take out your dreams. Instead, step out with confidence on faith.

There's No Such Thing as Can't

One of the lessons my parents taught me is I can do whatever I put my mind to. Another person may be better at it, but I can succeed at anything I want to do. I've followed this lesson throughout my life:

Math has never been my strong suite. But when I started my own business, one of the things I decided to do is maintain my own financial records and do my quarterly taxes. If you had told me in high school I would be doing that, I would have looked at you like you had lost your mind. But, as I did my homework before opening the business, I found that poor money management is one of the primary reasons a business fails. You *have to* know what's going on with your money. People have gone to jail because they let someone else handle the money, only to find out that the deductions their financial manager had taken were illegal. People (including athletes and entertainers who have made millions of dollars) have ended up broke because they turned their money management over to someone they trusted, and found out too late that the person was robbing them blind. I remember hearing Oprah Winfrey say in an interview that one of the best pieces of advice Bill Cosby gave her was to sign all her checks. I figured, if Oprah and Bill can do that (and they manage a much more complex financial empire than I do) I can, too.

While reading a program at an opera performance, I learned the story was based on a German fairytale. The thought crossed my mind that there are African and African American folktales that might make good operas. Some time later I came across information about an African whose life story just screamed "make me an opera." I had never written an opera, but, after thinking about it, I realized an opera is a play people sing. I had written plays. So I sat down and wrote the libretto (lyrics) and, later, found a wonderful composer (Neal Tate) to do the music.

When I was growing up, computers were huge things that filled up an entire room. I wrote my master's degree paper on a portable manual typewriter using carbon paper between two sheets of typing paper to make copies. On my first job, the company converted to electric typewriters. On my second job the company used word processors and, later, computers. I am not a technical person. It was a challenge each time I had to learn to use new equipment. I was fearful. I didn't understand how to make it work. It took me longer to get things done than when I used what I knew—a manual typewriter. But, I had no choice, so I made up my mind I would do what I had to do to learn how to use the equipment. I took classes. I asked questions. I experimented—using trial and error to learn what worked and what didn't work. Now, I not only type on the computer, but I design printed materials on the computer and know my way around the internet.

A former co-worker of mine who snow skied came back from a trip once and told me I should go on the trip the next year because it was a lot of fun. I'm afraid of heights, but the after-ski events sounded like so much fun I decided to go. When I found out what the trip cost I thought "I'm not paying that much just to party." So I took ski lessons. Skiing in Wisconsin and Upper Michigan wasn't bad; but the ski trip was to Montana, which had real mountains. On the trip, one of my ski club members (who was a very good skier and instructor) took the rookies out to help us sharpen our skills. One ski run, Calamity Jane, had a spot where all you could see was sky when you came around the corner. I knew there was ground on the other side of the rise, but when I saw nothing but sky, I panicked and fell. This happened over and over again throughout the day. Finally, my ski instructor said he couldn't help me get better until I learned to overcome my fear, go over the rise, and ski down the rest of the hill. He told me I didn't need to look at the whole mountain. I only needed to know what was 10 feet in front of my ski tips. For the next two days I went out by myself, trying to stay on my feet when I came to the scary part of Calamity Jane. The first day I fell every time. For half the next day I fell. But then I made up my mind I was going to make it down the hill on my feet. As I approached the section of Calamity Jane that made me panic, I looked down at my ski tips, looked about 10 feet ahead, took a deep breath and went over the rise and on to the other side. I made it all the way down the hill on my feet and started screaming and pumping my fists when I came to a stop. By the end of that week of skiing I had successfully come down all the easy runs and skied on some of the intermediate level runs. I've been skiing for more than 20 years—including some trips overseas. I'm certainly not ready for the Olympics, nor am I as good as some of the others in my ski club. But, I ski. There are still things that I don't do, but I never say I *can't* do them. I am convinced that, if I put my mind to it, I can do anything; and I believe anyone can do the same.

God made human beings able to reason, think, figure things out and innovate. What sets us apart from other animals is our ability to be creative—to look at situations and come up with a variety of solutions for dealing with them. So, don't let *can't* become part of your vocabulary. It's not about *can't*. It's about *how*.

FOCUS ON THE POSITIVE

Philippians 4:8 in the New Testament says "Finally, brethren, whatsoever things are true, whatsoever things are honest, whatsoever things are just, whatsoever things are pure, whatsoever things are lovely, whatsoever things are of good report; if there be any virtue, and if there be any praise, think on these things."

This statement, to me, is the prescription for living a contented life. There is no question things happen on a daily basis that can upset your day. But the secret to triumphant living is not to focus on negative things, but on positive things. That does not mean you deny the negative—you just don't dwell on it.

Scientists have discovered that our thoughts and attitudes create a physical reaction in our bodies. Negative thoughts and anger pump chemicals into our bloodstream that can damage our minds, our organs, and our nervous system; and cause our bodies to age faster. On the other side of the coin, positive thoughts and attitudes put chemicals in our bloodstream that help keep us healthy, heal our bodies when we do become sick, and keep us feeling and looking younger.

The benefits of positive thinking are not just related to health. Positive thinking can impact our lives overall. There are many incredible examples of the power of positive thinking. One of the most powerful in my mind is Nelson Mandela, who spent 27 years in prison for fighting against apartheid in South Africa. He lived in very brutal conditions. For much of the time his food was rationed. He was allowed one letter and one visitor every six months. He had to perform hard manual labor. Most people could easily understand how his circumstances might have made him a bitter man. But he *chose*, instead, to remain positive. He earned a bachelor of law degree while in prison. After his release he was elected the first post-apartheid president of South Africa. Instead of seeking revenge against those who mistreated him, he helped unite the country while seeking justice for past wrongs. Under his leadership South Africa made a peaceful transition from being the poster child for racial oppression to one that addressed human-rights violations without disintegrating into chaos and violence. His efforts helped him win the Noble Peace Prize.

While Nelson Mandela is world famous, there are many others whose names are not well known, but who also have succeeded against heavy odds. I think about my grandparents. On my mother's side of the family, my grandfather, born 25 years after the end of slavery, opened a funeral home that is still in the family. On my father's side, my great-grandfather, who worked in a sawmill in Forest, MS, owned enough land to create a family compound for himself and his children. He had a car with a driver, and was the person the town fathers (who were white) came to each year to put together the town budget. He was born two years after the end of slavery.

The common thread in the stories of men and women who overcome odds is they refuse to let negative thoughts and circumstances control their lives. As author and motivational speaker Zig Ziglar once said, "It is your attitude, not your aptitude, that determines your altitude."

If you want to live a triumphant life, think positively, set goals, and stay committed to doing what's necessary to achieve those goals. When you do that, anything is possible.

FOCUS ON SOLUTIONS

There's no way to get through life without experiencing problems and challenges. From the moment we're born, we're dealing with "issues." As infants, we have to cry to get the attention of a caregiver and let them know it's either time for a diaper change or food. As toddlers, we have to deal with how to get on our feet and walk without falling down, learn to tie our shoes, button our shirt or blouse and zip our coat. When we start school we have to learn to deal with a whole lot of new issues—reading, writing, math, following instructions, and getting along with other people.

As we get older we learn that people aren't always fair or honest. They don't always live by the Golden Rule: treat people the way they want to be treated. We learn that sometimes people who have fewer skills (and sometimes less education) than we do get opportunities we don't get. We learn that people will lie about you to keep you from getting something they want. We learn that people will take your kindness for weakness and try to use you. We learn that people will disappoint you.

How your life turns out depends not only on the issues you face, but also on how you deal with those issues. If you focus on the problem or the challenge—wondering why things happen, getting mad about things that happen, thinking about ways to get even with people for making things happen to you—there's a really good chance you won't achieve your dreams because your attention, energy and effort will be focused on the past rather than the future. The best way to deal with issues is to focus on what it will take to get past them, and move *toward* your life goals.

People who are successful are focused on solutions rather than problems. They concentrate on turning their obstacles into stepping stones. They learn from the situations they encounter and use that knowledge to move their lives forward. For them it's not about whether there's a mountain in front of them, it's about how they can get over, under, around or through that mountain. There is no *guarantee* they will get past that mountain, but there *is* a guarantee that if they don't make an effort, they won't have *any* success. By doing their best to overcome challenges, successful people make more progress in life than they might have otherwise. Two examples:

- Madam C.J. Walker, the daughter of a slave who was orphaned at age seven, lived in an abusive household and married at 14 to escape that household. She became the first African American female millionaire by building a business empire around hair care products for black women.

- John Johnson, who started the business empire that now publishes *Ebony* and *Jet* magazines, didn't have money to start his business. Banks would not lend him money. Instead of giving up his dream, he mapped out a plan for his business, and got his mother to use her furniture as collateral to get a $500 loan. To ensure the success of his business he got friends to go into stores and ask for his magazine, which convinced store owners to carry his publication. When he wanted to build an office in the Chicago Loop and the property owner wouldn't sell him the land because of his race, Johnson hired a white attorney to purchase the land and then built his office. Johnson worked hard, was determined, and refused to let anything or anyone keep him from succeeding. Born in poverty, he became one of the 400 riches men in the United States by focusing on solutions—how to get things done.

Life is not a smooth ride. As long as we're inhaling air, life will keep putting bumps on our road to success. The choice you have to make is whether you allow those bumps to dominate your life, or whether you do your best to move past them into a brighter future. The decision you make and the approach you take will play a critical role in determining whether you will be a victim or victor in life.

PIVOT

There's no rule that says you have to keep doing what you're doing—especially if what you're doing isn't moving your life in the direction you want it to go. Life is a journey. Along the way you make good decisions and bad decisions. The good ones, obviously, are ones you enjoy and want to repeat. The bad ones are ones you should learn from, do your best to move past, and not repeat.

It seems to me that moving past bad decisions was more common years ago. Back then most people would admit their mistakes and try to make amends—whether it was apologizing, making payments for damage done, doing community service work, or (worse case) serving jail time. Then they would try to chart a different course for their lives.

Lately it seems to me that too many people think when they make a bad decision they are stuck with the results for life. They don't seem to realize they can try to clean up the mess and move in another direction—that all hope of something better is not lost forever. As a consequence, they keep making bad decisions and digging a deeper and deeper hole that makes it difficult for them to get their lives back on a positive track. The result: they end up wasting their God-given gifts and potential.

Rather than becoming your own judge and jury, and condemning yourself to a life that is unproductive or (worse) destructive, follow the advice of American humorist and social commentator Will Rogers who said, "If you find yourself in a hole, stop digging." There are many examples of people who stopped digging and became productive.

Judge Greg Mathis

As a teenager, Judge Greg Mathis (who grew up in the Herman Gardens housing project in Detroit) followed his estranged father's lead by joining the notorious Errol Flynns street gang. He was arrested numerous times, and served time in the Wayne County Jail. His mother, who worked as a nurse's aide and housekeeper to support her four sons, visited him in jail one day to tell him she had colon cancer. He was 17.

Mathis was offered probation if he passed a GED exam within six months. He did, got out of jail and took a job at McDonalds—a job he had to keep to avoid violating probation and going back to jail.

A close family friend helped Mathis gain admission to Eastern Michigan University. He graduated with a bachelor's degree in public administration. He went to law school, but failed his bar exam once and was denied a license to practice several times because of his criminal background. But he did not give up.

Eventually he was elected a superior court judge for Michigan's 36th District, becoming the youngest superior court judge in the state. During his time in office he was rated one of the top five judges in the District.

After retiring from the bench, Judge Mathis started his own television show, which is syndicated and airs five days a week in most North America television markets.

His journey from juvenile delinquent to respected jurist and television personality has been chronicled in a play that toured the United States. Ballantine Books published his life story.

Cathy Hughes

After she became pregnant at age 16, Cathy Hughes (then Woods) married the baby's father, Alfred Liggins, Sr., before giving birth. The marriage lasted two years, and she found herself raising her child alone. Despite this challenge, she graduated from high school where she took business administration classes. In 1971 she got a job as an administrative assistant to Tony Brown, a noted commentator who founded Howard University's school of communications.

In 1973 Hughes was named general sales manager of Howard's WHUR-FM, and general manager two years later. After increasing the station's annual sales revenue from $300,000 to more than $3.5

million, Hughes left WHUR in 1978 to become vice president and general manager of WYCB Radio in Washington, D.C.

The following year, she and her second husband, Dewey Hughes, decided to buy their own radio station. They were rejected by 32 banks before they found a lender, and purchased WOL, a small Washington, D.C. station. They named their company Radio One. Hughes' second marriage ended shortly after purchasing the station.

Hard financial times forced Hughes and her son, Alfred Liggins, to move out of their apartment and into the radio station to make ends meet.

Radio One now owns and/or operates 53 stations in major markets across the country. In 2004 Hughes started a cable television network, TV One, that targets African Americans. In 2007 her son took over as CEO and President of Radio one. Hughes is the company's chairperson.

Chris Gardner

Chris Gardner lost most of his family's savings when he invested the money in medical equipment he thought would be the "next big thing." His wife left him and their toddler son in San Francisco and moved to New York City.

Gardner took a six-month *unpaid* internship at a Dean Witter brokerage firm hoping to become the one person out of *nineteen* candidates chosen to become a stockbroker. He and his son lived off what was left of their money in the bank until the government took their last $600 to cover unpaid taxes. Gardner and his son became homeless—at one point living in a train station bathroom. But he didn't give up. Gardner found a place for himself and his son to sleep at Glide Memorial United Methodist Church. To secure a spot each night he had to rush from work every day to be in line by 5 p.m.

Gardner's determination to get himself and his son back on solid economic ground paid off. He earned the job at Dean Witter, and became a successful stockbroker. Several years later he started his own investment firm—Gardner Rich & Co—and became a millionaire, motivational speaker and philanthropist.

What these individuals have in common is that when they faced challenges that were threatening to move their lives in a negative direction, they didn't keep moving in the same direction. They pivoted—turned in a new direction.

Someone once said the definition of insanity is to do the same thing over and over again and expect different results. I agree. If you're not happy with where you are in life, don't keep doing the same thing over and over again expecting different results. Pivot—plot a new course, and reinvent your life.

Playing the Hand You're Dealt

When I was in college one of the favorite pastimes among some students was playing a card game called Bid Whist, a game of strategy in which you and a partner play against two other players to win as many "books" (four cards per book) as possible.

The ultimate achievement in Bid Whist is to "run a Boston"—win every book—which means you win all the cards. Running a Boston isn't easy because you don't know which cards you will receive when they are dealt; and you don't know which cards any of the other players have in their hands—including your partner. To win you and your partner have to work as a team. The card your partner puts down is a signal to you about which cards he or she has in their hand. You also have to pay attention to the cards each member of the other team puts down to get an idea of which cards they have in their hands.

Running a Boston if you have a lot of winning cards in your hand is one thing. Doing it when you are evenly matched or have a poor hand (few winning cards) gives you real bragging rights because it means you and your partner had to out-think and out-play your opponents when the cards were, literally, stacked against you.

The game of Bid Whist offers a life lesson. It's not about the cards life deals you, it's about what you do with those cards: how you play the hand you're dealt to make the most out of your life.

If your family doesn't have a lot of money, that doesn't mean you have to be poor all of your life. You can focus on learning everything you can while you're in school, and getting the education you need to secure a good job or start your own business. If you make learning a life-long process by reading (articles and books about careers, about people who are successful and how they achieved their success, about current events so you know what's going on and how it affects you) you can stay on top of your game. Reading not only helps you keep up with what's going on, it also opens your mind to new ideas that can point you toward opportunities you might never have thought of before. Also, books can provide you with more detailed information than you might find on the internet.

If your family doesn't have a lot of money, you can also break the cycle of poverty by setting goals for yourself, developing a step-by-step plan for achieving those goals, and seeking out and learning from people who can help you achieve your goals. Setting goals is the first step toward developing a plan for your life—a plan that will help you do such things as find out where the opportunities are, what education and experience you need, who can help you, and how you should manage your money so you can enjoy life without being broke all the time. Without a plan, life just happens. That often leads to big disappointments because where you end up may not be where you hoped to be. Instead of looking back over your life and feeling good about what you see, you could easily end up wondering why things didn't turn out the way you thought they would.

If you don't get a job or promotion you think you should have, you don't have to get mad or give up. Instead, you can focus on learning everything you can on the job. Knowledge is power. By learning everything you can, you can become so good at what you do that if you don't get recognition in your current job, you can take your skills elsewhere. Whatever knowledge and skills you have when you leave one job give you an edge on your next job, or when you start a business. This is true now and will be more true in the future because the world economy (not just the economy in the United States) is increasingly based on information—what people know and what they can figure out. The ability to think strategically—to look at a situation, analyze it and figure out what to do to get the best results or achieve a goal—is worth its weight in gold; so is the ability to be creative—to come up with new ideas, products, services, and solutions to problems. In short, brainpower is the key to success, and those with the most brainpower will make the most money.

Playing the hand you're dealt applies to your personal life as well as your career. If you don't have movie star looks, don't try to look like the latest "it" girl or "hunk" to attract attention. Find your own style.

Dress in a way that is most flattering to you. Don't worry about whether it's the latest celebrity look. Everyone has something about them that's attractive. It could be your eyes or your hair or your smile. All of us are good-looking in our own way. What is even more important than outward appearances, however, is who you are inside and how you present yourself. If you are a positive, caring person who treats others the way you want to be treated, people will be attracted to that inner beauty.

If one of your life goals is to marry and have a family but, for some reason Mr. or Ms. Right never shows up, your life doesn't have to be empty and lonely. You can create a social network of people around things you enjoy doing, so you have people to do things with. You can find ways to make a positive difference in a child's life—whether it's by being a mentor, visiting schools, volunteering time and/or donating money to organizations that support children, working on issues that impact children's lives, sharing a smile, hello, kind word or encouraging a child in the neighborhood, being a foster parent, or adopting a child. The African proverb *"It takes a whole village to raise a child"* is true. When you help a child become his or her best self you are a parent, whether you are biologically related to that child or not.

In every aspect of your life, making the best of whatever cards life deals you helps you become a winner. As in Bid Whist, running a Boston (winning every card) is not an everyday occurrence. In fact, it is very unlikely that your life will go exactly the way you planned. But if you can look back and see more positive than negative—make one more book in the card game of life than you lost—then you've won.

WHEN LIFE GIVES YOU LEMONS,
MAKE LEMONADE

Each of us can point to negative experience in our lives—usually things others have done that hurt us or discourage us. It's human to be bothered by these experiences, but it's important not to let them dominate our existence. One of the people who did not let a horrific experience dominate his life was someone I had the privilege of knowing: Dr. James Cameron, founder of America's Black Holocaust Museum in Milwaukee, WI. We met as part of a writers' group called The New World Griots. In the tradition of the west African storytellers who preserved oral traditions and history, our group members read their work at various locations around Milwaukee. Dr. Cameron (Mr. Cameron at the time) was the historian and sage in our group. While the rest of us were reading poetry or short stories or excerpts from plays, he would read from his latest pamphlet recounting or commenting on some event in African American history. Though not trained as a historian, he was thorough and meticulous in his research.

It was not until he wrote his book, *A Time of Terror*, that the rest of us in the Griots knew what an amazing life Dr. Cameron had before we met him. He was one of three teenagers accused of murdering a white man in Marion, IN. The teens were arrested and jailed. A mob stormed the jail, beat them and lynched Dr. Cameron's two friends. The photo of that lynching, showing the hanging bodies and the lynch mob (made up of men, women *and* children, some of whom were smiling and pointing at the lynched youth) is one of the most famous photos in U.S. history. Dr. Cameron was supposed to be one of those hanging from the tree. But, as he told the story, a voice from the crowd shouted 'Let him go he's innocent,' and his life was spared. Even though he was not present when the crime occurred, James Cameron was sentenced to four years in state prison for being an accessory *before* the fact in the manslaughter case because he had been with the two other teens earlier in the evening. Dr. Cameron said he never knew who vouched for his innocence. Until his death at age 92, Dr. Cameron was the only known survivor of a lynching in U.S. history.

If anyone had a right to be bitter, angry and hostile, Dr. Cameron certainly did. But he did not allow that incident to set the tone for the rest of his life. Instead, he married, had a family, helped establish three National Association for the Advancement of Colored People (NAACP) chapters in Indiana, and served for eight years as the Indiana State Director of Civil Liberties where he investigated 25 incidents of civil rights infractions.

Dr. Cameron moved to Milwaukee after a growing number of death threats, and worked as a boiler engineer at Mayfair Mall. He wrote pamphlets on civil rights and racial injustice, and founded the Museum—the only one of its kind in the country—whose focus was not only on documenting injustices experienced by African Americans, but also " . . . providing visitors with an opportunity to rethink their attitudes and assumptions about race and racism."

Dr. Cameron was eventually pardoned by, and received an apology from Indiana Governor Evan Bayh. He was present in Washington, D.C. to receive an apology from the United States Senate for the federal government's failure to take action to stop the more than 5,000 lynchings that took place in the United States between the end of the Civil War and 1991. He received an honorary doctorate in humanities from the University of Wisconsin-Milwaukee in recognition of his work as a civil rights activist and founder of America's Black Holocaust Museum. He was interviewed by national and international media about his experience and, later, his museum.

While not sugarcoating what happened to him and (by extension) to thousands of other African Americans, Dr. Cameron preached the gospel of forgiveness *not* hate in his book and through his Museum. Because he chose to turn lemons (the near lynching experience) into lemonade (a positive, productive life) we have a better chance in this nation to come together as one people. The way Dr. Cameron lived his life—with courage and forgiveness—is an example, I think, we should all follow.

Nothing Beats a Failure But a Try

While most won't admit it, I believe many people don't get what they want out of life because they are afraid to try. As we get older, we either forget or reject some of the things we did in childhood—things that helped us successfully move from babyhood to toddler to childhood to young adulthood to adulthood.

We didn't give up on learning to feed ourselves when we were young, even when much of the food ended up on our face and our clothes. When we were learning to walk, we didn't stop trying the first time we lost our balance and sat down abruptly on our bottoms. In fact, we didn't give up at all. We just kept standing and moving our legs until we finally mastered the art of walking. Once we were up and moving, we explored the world around us to find out what was out there and how it worked. For our own protection, adults had to keep an eye on us to make sure we didn't hurt ourselves as we explored.

As older toddlers we became more independent. When someone tried to help us dress, we turned down their help because we wanted to dress ourselves. It might have taken us twice as long to do but when we were done, we were proud of ourselves. When someone tried to get us to do something we didn't want to do, we let them know in clear terms we didn't want to do it. We didn't always win the battle, but we did make our wishes known.

Those of us who became interested in playing sports didn't give up trying to master the sport's skills. We practiced more. Those of us who came to love reading didn't give up trying to understand those mysterious marks on the paper.

Somewhere along the way, too many of us have unlearned that stick-to-itiveness. We have lost that willingness and determination to try. Too often we let what other people say or think (or what we think they'll think) influence the direction of our lives.

It's human to want people to think well of you. It's human not to want to be embarrassed in front of other people. It's human not to want your shortcomings displayed for all the world to see. But progress only comes when you're willing to take chances, fail, learn from your mistakes, pick yourself up and try all over again.

Scientist and engineers know this well. When they are trying to create new products, processes, medications or equipment, understand how things work, or find answers to problems, they frequently hit a dead end or have things go wrong before they get it right. Many business people experience set-backs; and a significant number fail before they finally succeed.

The English poet John Keats once said "Don't be discouraged by a failure. It can be a positive experience. Failure is, in a sense, the highway to success, inasmuch as every discovery of what is false leads us to seek earnestly after what is true, and every fresh experience points out some form of error which we shall afterwards carefully avoid."

My junior high schools science teacher, Mr. Kaczmarek, said something similar as he passed out graded test papers: "The glory is not in never failing, but in picking yourself up every time you do." His comment has stayed with me all my life.

My ancestors and the ancestors of other African Americans lived in accordance with this idea long before I was a student in Mr. Kaczmarek's class. Those who grew up and died in slavery, and those who grew up and died in a segregated society, dreamed about a world that was much different from the one in which they lived. They dreamed a world in which their children, grandchildren, great-grandchildren, or great-great-grandchildren would have an opportunity to live with dignity, go to the school of their choice, and get as much education as they wanted. They dreamed of a world where future generations would have no limits on what they could achieve in life—a world in which they could live comfortably in a nice house and have ample food and clothing. Some may even have dreamed that one day this country would elect an African American President of the United States.

But they did more than dream. They worked hard to keep their family together. Though they may have had little formal education themselves, they built schools, colleges and universities, churches, businesses and mutual aid societies to help uplift themselves and those who would follow. They invented traffic lights and machinery to sew the soles and tops of shoes together. They performed the first open heart surgery. They helped survey and lay out Washington, D.C. They invented a device to reduce the number of train collisions. They developed a system for storing blood plasma that made blood banks possible. They modernized the design of the clothes iron and invented the straightening comb. They created the jazz and blues music that is universally recognized as America's original musical art form. They created art and literature to preserve African American culture. They fought in wars against tyranny (beginning with the Revolutionary War), *and* a war for equal justice at home. And they often did these things in the face of life-threatening conditions with much fewer resources and rights than we have today. They were not afraid to try new things, to test the limits society tried to place on them, to push for equal rights, justice, and an equal opportunity. If those who came before us were not afraid to try what seemed impossible, we have no excuse for being afraid to try. We have no excuse for becoming discouraged if we don't succeed right away.

When you find yourself doubting whether you can accomplish something, think about those who came before you, and the obstacles they had to overcome to lay the groundwork for the world you live in today. Remember the philosophy that carried them through: "Nothing beats a failure but a try."

Each New Day Is
Filled With Opportunity

I'm not certain what it is about human beings, but it seems many of us spend a lot of our time looking back at what happened in the past that didn't go the way we thought it should. We feel regret. We feel disappointment. We feel shame. We let the past color the present and the future. Doing that, I believe, puts limits on our ability to focus on what we *can* do. As a result, we don't achieve and contribute as much as we could in and to life.

Instead of getting caught up in what happened in the past or what is not working, we should focus on what we have. There is a story that has been around for years about a poor man who complained because he had no shoes—until he met a man who had no feet. Are you in good health? Do you have a house to live in? Are you able to eat regularly and get enough to eat? Do you have *real* friends who care about you and are there in good times and bad? Do you have a family that cares about you and has your back? If so, you are blessed.

Instead of focusing on the past, we should see each new day as one filled with opportunity. We can't change the past. We are not promised the next day. We can only have an impact on today. What we do with the time we have now determines whether we will be satisfied or disappointed with the way our life is going; and will determine whether we leave the world a better place than it was before we got here. Are you working to make yourself a better person? Are you using the talent God gave you for your benefit *and* the benefit of others? Are you behaving in a way that will make a difference in the lives of others? Have you taken time to enjoy the life you have—as imperfect as it may be—and counted your blessings?

Think of your life as a big canvas on which you get to paint the picture of who you are and what you've done. Each day you are alive you get to change the way that picture looks. Some days you may paint a whole scene. Other days you may only be able to put one stroke of color on the canvas. The important thing each day is to think about what you want your final picture to look like after you're gone. At our core, all of us want the picture to be beautiful. Being aware of the type of image you are presenting of yourself each day gives you a better chance to create a beautiful finished picture.

American theologian Reinhold Niebuhr described this process another way when he wrote what has become known as *The Serenity Prayer:* "God grant me the serenity to accept the things I cannot change; courage to change the things I can; and wisdom to know the difference."

As you go through life, instead of boo-hooing or becoming uptight about what is or is not happening in your life, think about this prayer. Then re-focus your attention on trying to be the best "you" you can be; and on being a blessing to others.

It's Not Always Easy
Keeping Your Shoulders Squared

It's not always easy to keep your head up and your shoulders squared. Life can deal you body blows that shake your self-confidence and make you want to put your head down and slump over. Often those blows come in the form of disappointments at the hands of other people who may:

- Act like they're your friend and then talk about you behind your back.
- Say they care about you and then abandon you when you need them the most.
- Listen to your dreams and then slowly pick them apart until you begin to doubt whether your idea makes sense, or whether *you* have what it takes to make your dreams come true.
- Try to make you over in *their* image of who you should be, and then laugh about how ridiculous you are for trying to be something you're not.
- Tell you what a good job you're doing at work and then undercut you to make you look bad to your boss.

I sometimes wonder why people do things like this. While it's frustrating, aggravating and disappointing to be subjected to this behavior, and having to deal with it can make you angry, it's important to try not to dwell on what other people do. Instead, try to move past their actions and live the best life you can:

- **Remind yourself when you're under attack that you may be doing something right or innovative.** People usually don't attack you when you're going along with the program, or doing the same old thing. It's when you're non-traditional that you draw negative attention. (For example: when you're a geek instead of a member of the *cool crowd*, you enjoy school/get good grades, pick a non-traditional career, like classical or jazz music, don't drink, dress conservatively, stand up for what you think is right rather than what's popular.) The people who helped change the course of human history in a positive way are not the ones who refused to step off the beaten path. They are the ones who dared to be different, and blazed a new path.

- **Cut ties with people who undercut you.** If someone does this, don't assume it's an accident. Assume it's intentional, and don't allow that person to be part of your life. If the person is a co-worker—someone you can't avoid—minimize your contact with them. Just do what you need to do with them for your job. Document everything you do in writing so you have proof of what you are and are not doing.

- **Make sure you don't give people ammunition to use against you by telling them all your business.** People who are not happy with where they are in *their* lives can get jealous in a minute if they see you succeeding. I've had people I thought were good friends turn on me, so I make sure I'm very careful about disclosing too much personal information. I'm not paranoid about it. I just don't talk about everything with everybody. Remember, just because someone shows their teeth in what look like a smile, it doesn't mean they're your friend. The wolf in the story *Little Red Riding Hood* showed his teeth just before he jumped out of bed and tried to kill her. When you encounter someone who is always smiling in your face, keep a watchful eye on what else they're doing to determine whether they are sincere or just pretending.

- **Remind yourself that "God don't make no junk."** No one is perfect. All of us have room for improvement. But, no one is a total disaster, either. There's a song by Rev. James Cleveland that says, "Please be patient with me, God is not through with me yet. When God gets through with me, I shall come forth like pure gold." We are all works in progress—including those who are putting us down. It's o.k. to think about what those individuals have to say to determine whether there is something you *can* learn from their comments. Sometimes other people can help us see things about ourselves we need to improve. But if you find that someone has *nothing* positive to say about you, the chances are they are trying to be destructive, not helpful, and it's time to put distance between them and you. While we all should try to be better today than we were yesterday, we don't have to tolerate people whose mission is to cut us down to size.

- **Take time to get away from people.** Alone time (even if it's just for an hour or two) is helpful. Alone time could be a movie, going to the mall, lakefront or park, walking around by yourself, sitting under a tree and reading a book, sitting in a room and looking out the window, taking time to think. The key is to have some time when you do not have to talk and interact with anyone. Alone time is also a great time to listen for that inner voice—God—to give you directions on where you need to go next, and what you need to do next in your life. Finding the path you're supposed to be on by spending time alone to listen to that inner voice helps lead to a more satisfying life.

- *Make time* **to do things you like to do; that make you feel good about yourself.** It doesn't have to be anything spectacular. It could be going to a sports event or participating in a sport. It could be going to a play or a concert or participating in some other arts activity. It could be volunteering with an organization to help others. It could be cooking. It could be making something with your hands. It could be cleaning or redecorating. It could be reading. It could be going for a walk. Taking time for fun makes you feel peaceful and helps balance out the stresses in life.

- **Look back at what you've accomplished so far in life.** Most of us accomplish more than we think, but we are so busy "doing" that we don't take time to reflect on where we started and where we are now. Seeing progress and improvement in our lives reminds us we are capable people—even if others try to tell us otherwise.

- **Remember what others mean for evil, God will turn to good (as long as you're doing what He wants you to do).** You plus God can beat any opponent.

- **Remember that what goes around comes around.** Martin Luther King said the arc of the universe is long but it bends toward justice. In the end, the good guys will win and the bad guys will pay for their misdeeds.

- **Read books about others who have overcome obstacles not only for inspiration, but also for ideas you can use in your own situation.** Reading these books can also help put life situations in perspective. The obstacles others had to overcome can make your problems look small by comparison, and help remind you how blessed you've been throughout your life.

- **Think about your ancestors who did what they could to give you a better life.** I think about my slave ancestors who, with no reason for hope, never gave up on their dream that one day their children or their children's children would live a better life. They laid the foundation for me to live a comfortable, fulfilling and productive life. So, I have no reason to stand with my head down and my shoulders slumped. I am a descendant of the survivors—the ones who didn't give up. I have no excuse for not standing tall and proud. I have no excuse for not believing that anything is possible. I have no excuse for not trying to achieve my dreams.

Whenever I feel discouraged, I remember something I first heard in childhood that is a variation on two Bible versus (Ecclesiastes 9:11 and Mark 13:13): 'The race is not given to the swift, nor to the strong, but to the one who endures to the end.' Then I pick up my head, square my shoulders and move on with life.

CLIMBING OUT OF THE VALLEY

No matter how upbeat a person you are, you will have times when all you want to do is lay in bed with the covers pulled over your head. It's natural. Nobody is happy all the time.

Sometimes figuring out the reason for your funk is easy: the death of a loved one, the break-up of a relationship, a setback in achieving your dream, financial problems. Other times, there is no apparent reason for it.

When the source of feeling down isn't apparent, it's time to slow down and take inventory of what's happening in your life. There are any number of things that can affect your state of mind:

Your body could be telling you it's not doing well

- You may not be getting enough rest. Because you're so busy you might get less than six hours of sleep a night, or you might wake up during the night because you're concerned about a problem. If you're gasping for air, you many have sleep apnea or some other breathing disorder that needs immediate medical treatment.
- You many not be eating the kind of food your body needs to stay healthy and strong. You may, for example, be eating too many foods high in fat, salt or sugar, and may not be drinking enough water. A balanced diet includes fruits, vegetables, whole grains, foods rich in calcium (such as milk, yogurt, cottage cheese,

collard greens, fortified soy milk, beans), and foods high in protein and lower in fat (such as fish, chicken and turkey). Dietary guidelines published by the U.S. Department of Health and Human Services and the U.S. Department of Agriculture list the kind and amount of food people need daily to maintain a healthy body and weight.

- You may not be getting enough daily exercise. Exercise doesn't have to happen at a gym or in a class. You can walk more, take the stairs instead of the elevator, find a sport you enjoy, spend less time watching television and more time doing activities you enjoy that get your body moving.

- You may not be taking enough time to relax and enjoy life. If all you do is study, work, eat and sleep, that can wear your body out. You need time to do things that don't have a deadline so you can reduce the stress in your life. Unplug the earphones and the music, and listen to what your heart is telling you about what you want from life.

Your sub-conscious mind may be telling you something is not right in your life.

- You may be hanging around with what I call human storm clouds—people who make you feel bad when you are around them. If someone is always talking about what's not right in the world, their constant negativity can bring your spirits down. If they are always telling you what's wrong with you, and never have anything positive to say, that can wear on your self-confidence. If you talk with them about this behavior and they aren't willing to change, it's time to stop allowing them to be part of your life.

- You may be doing something to please others that you don't really want to do or feel uncomfortable doing. Often this happens when someone is trying to be popular. The world is filled with all kinds of people. Instead of following the crowd, start your own crowd by finding others who like doing things you enjoy.

- You may be putting too much pressure on yourself—trying to do too much or be perfect. There are 24 hours in a day. Some of that time is taken up by school or work, sleep, eating and other daily personal matters. If you're fortunate, you have 4-6 hours left in the day to do things that aren't "required." It's important to establish priorities for what you want to do with that time. That doesn't mean scheduling every minute. It does mean understanding what's really important to you so you can look at the choices you face everyday and decide whether they're helping you get where you want to be in life, or making a difference in the lives of others.

- You may be experiencing changes in your life that concern you or make you unhappy. For example, you may be nervous about moving to a new neighborhood, city, school or job. If so, learn as much as you can about the new place *before* you move so you can start identifying where you fit in. You may *feel* a need to change your life, but don't know exactly what you want to do. Take time to think about what you want to be doing in the next five years, and what it will take to get there. Put together an action plan or checklist *in writing* that tells you what you need to do each day, week, or month to get there. Go over that plan or checklist at least monthly to make sure you're on track. Identify and connect with people who can help you achieve your goal.

You may be facing situations in your family that concern you or make you unhappy.

- Someone in your family may be sick. There are organizations you can contact to help you learn more about the illness and find out where you can get help and treatment for your family member. There are organizations that focus on just about any disease and illnesses human beings have. The American Cancer Society, Diabetes Association, American Heart Association are among the more well known, but there are many, many more. The public library and the internet are also good places to find information about local and national health organizations. When using the internet, make sure you're visiting a site that is not simply a business (.com, .biz). Sites that end in .org, .edu or .gov are more likely to provide information that is not slanted to make you buy a particular product or service. Finally, the National Institutes of Health (a division of the U.S. Department of Health and Human Services) has information that can answer almost any question imaginable. The information is arranged by the different parts of the body and systems (such as the immune system, blood system, nervous system), making it easier to find what you need to know.

- You may be experiencing conflicts in the family. There are organizations and social service agencies that can help you identify where to get help and treatment for everything from domestic, child, and elder abuse to drug, alcohol and gambling addiction to mental health services and more. Again, the public library, internet and National Institutes of Health can help you find information and assistance related to whatever the issues are.
- You may have financial pressures impacting your family. If too much debt is the problem, there are *non-profit* consumer credit counseling organizations that can provide information and assistance. If unemployment is the issue, look for help at *non-profit* job centers or employment counseling agencies. Local community or technical colleges and government offices may also be able to provide some direction—especially if training is necessary. The public library has books, other materials, and research resources on the internet that can provide career and job hunting tips. The internet is a good place to find information. (Again, focus on sites that end in .org, .edu. or .gov.)

Taking action to do something about a problem—being proactive—will help reduce the feeling of helplessness that can cause stress and depression, and help pull you out of your funk.

When what's happening is more than you can deal with, seek help from a person who can talk you through the situation. That person needs to be someone who is trustworthy, knowledgeable and good at thinking things through and coming up with positive solutions (solutions that don't make matters worse). Often those individuals work for organizations and agencies that specialize in whatever the issue is you're trying to address. Churches (the faith community) are another resource. In addition to whatever counseling they may offer, a faith community can provide spiritual and moral support through prayer and being a caring presence.

Sometimes the funk is so deep it is important to get professional help by visiting a counselor, social worker, psychologist or psychiatrist to overcome the down feeling. The bottom line is don't allow "the blues" to become a constant state of being. Staying in the valley of despair and hopelessness too long is when the real trouble begins.

You Are Never Alone.
God is Always With You

There are times when you find yourself caught between despair and desperation. Just when you thought you were about to get the thing you wanted most in life, it starts slipping away from you. People you thought would be there for you are no where to be found. Nothing is going right.

It's at times like this that it would be easy to give up hope, to think things will never get better, to wonder why this is happening to you. The truth of the matter is that "bad" things do happen to good people. None of us are immune to that. But God is always there, ready to bring you through.

It took me a while to learn this. While I've always been a practicing Christian, it took a while to develop a personal relationship with God—to understand that He was not just a theoretical being in the sky, but someone real who is a friend in the time of need.

My first real understanding came when He delivered me from a stress-inducing work situation that landed me in the emergency room. I told God I couldn't handle it any more and turned the situation over to Him. He removed the people who were creating the stress from my life by having some transfer to other departments and others leave the company. My latest understanding came when a work project forced me to cancel a planned (and paid for) ski trip. At first I was annoyed. I was able to get most of my money back, and was resigned to not doing something I had been looking forward to. But soon I realized the true reason for that cancellation. My father, who had been reasonably healthy (despite his dementia) suddenly took ill around his birthday. Because I was in town, I was able to assess the situation, and get in contact with my brother who flew in from California. Together we helped my mother make decisions and get things in order.

Less than a month after his birthday, my father died. Being at home in Milwaukee allowed me to be at his bedside when he died, and to be there for my mother who, otherwise, would have had to face that situation alone.

As a human being, I forget on occasion that God has everything under control. But I've lived long enough to see many instances in which He has either kept me from doing something really stupid or gotten me out of a mess. As I'm tensing up and starting to worry in the midst of the latest storm, I remind myself that He hasn't missed a beat yet—that no matter how bad it may seem, I am not alone. I remember I've got the ultimate "A Team" on my side—that even in tough times I have a partner who will be with me through thick and thin and won't let me down. Then, I let go and let Him handle it.

WHAT GOES AROUND, COMES AROUND

There's an old saying from down South: "What goes around, comes around." What this means is if you do something evil, something evil will happen to you. If you do something good, something good will happen to you. I've found this to be true.

As the Chair of the Milwaukee Metropolitan Sewerage District during the construction of a $2.1 billion deep tunnel project, I was part of the negotiating team trying to reach a deal with some suburban communities that disagreed about how much money they should pay for this project. The negotiations went on for months and used up a lot of my time. We would get to a point where it looked like we were going to work things out, and then the suburban negotiating team would come up with another problem or condition they needed us to agree to before they would sign a contract.

I owned a small business and lost a lot of money during that time because I wasn't able to work. One day after a negotiating session, a person who worked for one of the firms representing the other side met me in the hallway and told me the suburban negotiating team's strategy was to string out the process as long as possible until I was forced out of business. I turned that battle over to God and kept doing my job as the District Chair. Eventually an agreement was reached. I was still in business. But a year or so later one of the lead people on the suburban negotiating team had to close his business.

Things like this have happened throughout my life. God either stops things that people do from creating harm, or turns negative intentions to my benefit. So, I have learned not to waste a lot of time and emotional energy worrying about the actions of others. I know as long as I'm trying to do the right thing, what goes around, comes around.

LIVING WELL IS THE BEST REVENGE

In the Old Testament story of Joseph and his coat of many colors, Joseph's brothers (who were jealous of him because they thought their father loved him more, and because he was a dreamer) considered killing Joseph but decided, instead, to sell him into slavery. Joseph ended up in Egypt where his ability to dream and interpret dreams accurately caught the attention of the Pharaoh. The Pharaoh was so grateful and impressed by Joseph's skill that he made him a governor in Egypt. Because Joseph had predicted a famine and persuaded the Pharaoh to stockpile food, the people of Egypt had more than enough to eat when the famine came.

People from other countries—including Joseph's family—didn't do as well, and were forced to come to Egypt to buy grain. Joseph was in charge of food distribution. When his brothers showed up he recognized them immediately, but they didn't recognize him. Joseph told his brothers who he was, which freaked them out because they thought he would try to get back at them. Instead of punishing them for what they had done to him, Joseph realized God had sent him to Egypt to be in position to help his family and others from his country when the famine came.

When the Pharaoh heard Joseph's family was struggling in their homeland, he invited the family to move to Egypt and gave them the best land to live on.

Joseph's story offers a number of life lessons:

- **People will sometimes turn on you—even those you thought were friends; even members of your family.** They may do this because they are jealous, or because you don't conform to *their* idea of who you should be. I don't know why this is. Perhaps it's because they don't know how to deal with someone that doesn't fit the mold; or perhaps they're frustrated because seeing you follow your dreams reminds them they haven't followed theirs.

- **Don't let the negative actions of others ruin your life.** Joseph did not try to hide the gift of interpreting dreams God gave him. Instead, he used that gift to make a difference in the lives of others.

- **Faced with the choice between love and forgiveness or hated and revenge, choose love and forgiveness.** Given what his brothers did to him, Joseph could easily have used his power to punish them, but he didn't. Instead he used his power to help his family and others.

- **It is not the people who conform to the world who change history; it is the dreamers—those who, in the words of George Bernard Shaw, " . . . dream things that never were and ask 'why not?' "** The "why not" people are often ahead of their time. They see life differently—see possibilities or new ways of doing things that others don't.

- **Living well is the best revenge.** The British philosopher Edmund Burke once said "He who wrestles with us strengthens our nerves and sharpens our skill. Our antagonist is our helper." What I believe he meant is this: Every time you overcome a problem or obstacle someone places in your way, you become stronger and more confident. It hurts to be rejected or betrayed. But remember, despite his brothers' best efforts, Joseph was the one who ended up living in a palace and helping to run a powerful country.

THE TOUGHER THE BATTLE, THE SWEETER THE VICTORY

When you're in the middle of a tough situation and you're trying to work your way through it, it's no fun. It may not be apparent as you go through hard times, but often some good comes from the experience. Every tough situation teaches you lessons that can help you become a stronger and smarter person. Those lessons include learning:

- **To recognize trouble when you see it.** If you think about how you ended up in the situation in the first place, you can avoid making the same mistake.

- **What works and what doesn't work.** As you work your way through a problem you can learn what works so you can repeat it, and what doesn't work so you won't do it again.

- **The people you can and cannot count on when times are tough.**

- **Where you can get help.**

While it is better to think things through *before* taking action so you won't find yourself in tough situations, sometimes that doesn't happen. Taking a wrong turn doesn't mean you've hit a dead end or that nothing good can happen to you. If you focus on learning from your mistakes and move in a different direction, you can turn the page to a new and better chapter in your life's story. Every time you successfully deal with a tough problem, you gain confidence in your ability to overcome obstacles. Those victories over adversity make life sweeter.

WHAT COUNTS MOST IS HOW YOU FINISH

I love watching the Olympics—not just for the drama of athletic competition, but also because there always seems to be a story that speaks to the power of the human spirit, captures your heart and teaches a life lesson.

A number of years ago I was watching a track and field competition on television. The field of runners included a young man from England. Like his competitors, he had trained for years for this moment. He had competed against the best in the world at his event to qualify for the privilege to represent his country. This was the moment he had been waiting for—his moment in the sun to show off his talent. As the runners turned the corner into the home stretch, he was still in the competition. Suddenly he pulled up lame and fell to the ground. He got up and tried to continue running, but the pain was too intense. His father came down out of the stands, draped his son's arm around his shoulder, and helped him hobble across the finish line. The crowd roared their appreciation for his determination.

At the Atlanta Olympics, I was sitting in the stands watching distance runners compete. The race for the medals ended. All the competitors left the track, except for one man who continued to run around the track. When the crowd saw that he was running not to win, but to complete the task he had trained so hard for, they started to cheer. When he made the final lap and crossed the finish line with his hands raised up, the crowd rose and gave him a standing ovation. Some of the competitors who had finished the race earlier were also there to greet him when he finished.

At the 1988 Winter Olympic games, Jamaica sent a bobsled team to compete. Now, unless it happened during the Ice Age, I don't think Jamaica has ever had snow. Nonetheless, the team was there. The young men (members of the Jamaican military) had been approached by two Americans with family and business ties to Jamaica to form a Jamaican bobsled team. The Americans had seen pushcart derby races on the island, and realized the skills were similar to those needed for bobsledding. The team was coached by a New York state native. At first the idea of a Jamaican bobsled team was treated as a joke by commentators and news media. But as the competition started, it became apparent that these men were very serious about what they were doing, and had put in the time and effort to be competitive. The snickering stopped. The team became *the* story of the games. While they did not win a medal, a Hollywood movie was later made about them.

Though none of these competitors earned Olympic medals for their effort, they earned the respect and admiration of their peers and the spectators. They may not have been "winners" based on receiving a gold, silver or bronze medal, but they were winners in life. They set a goal for themselves to compete in the Olympics, achieved that goal, and performed to the best of their ability. What counted most was not how they started out, but how they finished.

STAYING FOCUSED

LIFE TEACHES YOU LESSONS

Life is about lessons—some positive, some negative. The positive lessons teach you what to do. The negative lessons teach you what *not* to do. If you don't allow the negatives to discourage you, these lessons will strengthen you.

You can't get through life without experiencing some negatives. Even "good" people who are trying to do the right thing will experience negatives. You don't have to learn everything from personal experience. You can learn from observation—seeing what others do and the impact their decisions have on their lives.

How your life turns out is not so much determined by what happens to you, but by how you deal with it. Some people let minor setbacks—like not getting the recognition they think they deserve, or having someone say negative things about them—throw them into a tailspin. A news broadcast on television included an excerpt from a speech Oprah Winfrey gave to students during Howard University's graduation ceremonies. In that segment she talked about how the people at the television station where she worked early in her career told her she would not be successful in television. They told her she needed to change her name because nobody would remember it. They moved her from her news job into a talk show job to give her something to do until her contract ran out. She could easily have let that discourage her, but she didn't. The rest, as they say, is history.

Pay attention to life's lessons. Learn from both the positive and the negative. Commit yourself to turning every experience—even the bad ones—to your benefit; and share these benefits with others to make a difference in their lives. By doing this the positives will out weigh the negatives and you will live a fuller, more productive, more satisfying and, ultimately, more triumphant life.

You Can Learn From Everyone

I once heard a professional athlete say no one could tell him anything. My immediate reaction was, "Man, you could be headed for some serious trouble." What he *may* have meant was that he's capable of thinking for himself. But if he really meant what he said—that he knows it all, and doesn't need input from anyone else—there's a real chance his life will move off in a direction he didn't intend for it to go.

One of the most dangerous things you can do is think you know it all—that you're invincible. When you think no one can tell you anything, you shut off your critical thinking skills—your ability to analyze a situation and determine what's the best thing to do. When you act like no one has anything worthwhile to tell you, you run the very real risk of missing out on an important message or opportunity that God is trying to send you through another person. You should pay attention to what others say to you. If you hear the same "advice" over and over again from different people at different times, it could be God sending you an important message. By missing this message, you could find your life spiraling off in directions you hadn't planned for it to go. The truth is, no matter how long you live, how smart you are, how much knowledge you gain, you can still learn from everyone you meet.

Having said this, I don't mean you should shut your brain down and do whatever people tell you to do. Even when you hear the same message over and over, be sure to analyze it to determine whether you are being lead to do something positive or negative, legal or illegal, beneficial or harmful. People come into your life for a variety of reasons. The key is to determine what that reason is. Some of those people are there to show you what to do. Others are there to show you what *not* to do. I use the word "show" intentionally because the message they're giving you won't necessarily be spoken. They may be delivering the message through their actions or through what happens to them because of their actions. You can discover the underlying messages in what people say or do by paying attention to what is happening in their lives. Are they better off or worse off because of their actions? Are they enjoying life, or are they always complaining, talking about what they don't have, or searching for something better?

Make a conscious effort to learn from the lives of others. If you want a successful career, read about, talk to and observe someone who is successful in the field you want to enter. If your goal is financial security, learn how to manage your money by reading about, talking to and observing those who are living comfortably—especially in their retirement years. Read books about money management and investment. Read business newspapers and magazines. Watch and listen to programs on public television and public radio that talk about finance and investment. If you want to earn the respect of others, read about, talk to and observe what those who are highly respected in the community and throughout history do or did. By learning from others, you can increase the likelihood you will be successful, and reduce the amount of drama in your life.

You Don't Get Where You Are in Life by Yourself

Every culture has its core values—the principles upon which everything else is built. One of the core values in this country is the idea that anyone can achieve whatever they want in life through determination and effort. This value is called rugged individualism. There is even a fictional character in American literature that serves as the prototype for this value—Horatio Alger, who grew up poor, managed to pull himself up by his bootstraps, and became a successful and wealthy person. His story was the example my classmates and I heard about when teachers wanted to motivate us to do our best.

I believe this country does offer more opportunities for anyone to climb the ladder of success than most places in the world. This is especially true for females. But I also know from personal experience and observation as well as from studies done by scholars that the playing field is not level. I also know from experience and observation that no one—not even those who claim they did it by themselves—really got where they are without help from someone or a number of someones. All of us are where we are because someone either directly helped us get there, or laid the foundation for us to get there.

My ancestors, who were brought to this country in chains and were legally enslaved for nearly three hundred years, decided that lifestyle wasn't working for them. They dreamed a world that would be better for their children and grandchildren, and worked to make that dream come true. Contrary to most historic accounts, many enslaved Africans were not passively waiting for someone to set them free. They took action to help free themselves, their families and others.

My grandparents—who spent nearly all their lives living under legal segregation—worked hard and created businesses that allowed them to comfortably support their children; and they encouraged their children to get an education—something that, during slavery, could get you whipped and/or killed.

My parents, both college graduates, not only told me I could be anything I wanted to be in life, but exposed me to many options so I would have a world of opportunities to choose from. We had a set of the *World Book Encyclopedia* in the house. In addition to receiving toys like dolls and a tea set for Christmas, I received toys like a chemistry set and a red and blue plastic printing press. When, as a high school student, I mentioned I might want to become a psychologist, my father joined the Psychology Book Club so I could get a head start reading and learning about the field.

Others who were not members of my family helped pave the way for me to become whatever I chose to be. Thousands of people put their lives on the line during the modern Civil Rights movement in the 1950s and 60s to end legal segregation, and open doors to careers that children like me might never have considered before. In elementary school, my principal, Miss Henrietta K. Hardy, saved me from physical and permanent psychological harm inflicted by classmates who started waiting for me daily after school to beat me up because I got good grades. She let me sit in her office for as long as it took for the crowd to leave. In junior high school, my music teacher, Ralph Ullenberg, told me after a music appreciation class that I was going to play the violin. He sent information to my parents about how to make that happen. It opened up the world of classical music to me.

Throughout my work career I have had mentors who opened up doors for me. Ron Martin hired me out of college to be a reporter for *The Miami Herald*—at that time one of the country's top 10 newspapers. Tom Shropshire helped guide my career at Miller Brewing Company, where I became a manager and learned what I know about running a top-notch business. Linda Stewart, someone I barely knew at the time, got me a job running a business development program in the University of Wisconsin—Milwaukee (UWM) School of Business, which allowed me to help others start successful businesses and provided me with a pension that I live on now. Another Ron Martin helped me navigate the university culture while I ran the program. Roy Evans, who was familiar with my marketing and business skills, recommended me to a state senator who was running for Congress. When she won I was hired to work in her District Office, where I use my small business development skills to help others create jobs.

Certainly, I had to prepare myself for these opportunities; and I had to be willing to take advantage of the opportunities. But others laid the foundation for those opportunities. As I continue to grow and develop and explore new options in life, I don't "get the big head," because I know I stand on the shoulders of many people who boosted me up. And, I know that undergirding all of this is God, who always has my back. I pay back my debt for the help I have received by reaching back to help others achieve their goals.

You Don't Have to Learn Things the Hard Way

There are many reasons people make the wrong turn in life. A big one, I believe, is their immediate environment may not offer examples of other ways to do things and live their lives. If everybody you know is doing and saying the same things and acting the same way, it's easy to think that's the way the whole world is.

But, you *don't have to* travel the same road—especially if that road leads to a bad outcome. For example, if you see someone burn their hand on a stove, you don't have to put your hand on the stove to know it's hot. If you see people who abuse drugs and alcohol living a tough life on the street, going to jail and dying young, you don't have to abuse drugs and alcohol to know substance abuse is a bad idea. If you see people who have dropped out of high school struggling to make ends meet because they can't get a good paying job, and see those who have graduated from high school and gone on to get additional education in college or a trade and technical school living better, you don't have to drop out of high school to know having a good education is key to a better life—especially now when the competition for jobs is *from people living in countries all over the world.* If you see a teen mother struggling to take care of herself and her baby, or a teen mother or father having to give up hanging out with their friends because she (or he) has parental responsibilities, you don't have to have a child early in life to figure out you need to be able to financially and emotionally support yourself and a child *before* you have one.

As you look at what other people are doing and the impact their actions have on their lives, ask yourself "Is that *really* where I want to be?" If the answer is "no," start looking beyond your immediate surroundings to find examples of other options. Look for those in the community who are taking a different, more productive path out of what may be difficult circumstances, and connect with them. In school, look for teachers, administrators, counselors and coaches who are willing to help you prepare yourself for a better life. In the library look for librarians, books, videos and other media that can help you learn about other life options, expand your view of what's possible in the world, and find resources that can help you chose the best options for achieving what you want in life. On the job, look for co-workers, supervisors and (especially in smaller businesses) business owners who are willing to not only show you how to do your job, but also show you how to get to the next level. In the media, look for programs on public television, public radio and cable television that show you a world beyond the one you are most familiar with (not just the glitz and glamour world, but the world of history, biography, ideas, science, travel, arts and culture). In the community, look for volunteer opportunities with organizations where you can help others and learn about solutions to problems. In church, look for people who are trying to live by a positive set of rules, and are making a difference in the world.

Not everyone you come in contact with will be helpful to you. It's rare that you connect with the first person you choose. But don't give up. There are those who are willing to make a difference in your life. Keep trying until you find someone willing to give you the time and support you need to move your life in a positive direction. There *is* someone out there. You don't have to learn things the hard way.

OLDER PEOPLE ARE NOT IRRELEVANT

Ever since the 1960s when someone came up with the phrase "never trust anyone over 30," there has been a bias against people who are considered too old to be card-carrying members of popular culture. Some consider the older generation irrelevant—believing what older people say and think doesn't matter. Others think what older people have to say worked in bygone days, but doesn't apply today.

This attitude reminds me of high school where you had the in crowd and the outcasts. The in crowd was made up of popular kids—the ones everyone thought were "cool." The outcasts were the kids everyone thought were "square"—most often the nerdy kids. The problem with this division—whether it's based on age or on popularity—is that it cuts people off from others who might be able to help them get where they want to be in life.

In his poem *For Whom the Bell Tolls*, clergyman John Donne wrote "no man is an island, entire of itself." That goes for women, too. By connecting with the *right* older people, each of us can become more knowledgeable, stronger, positive and productive human beings. To identify the *right* older person, you need to pay attention to what they're telling you to do. If someone is telling you to do something that could lead to trouble or move your life in a direction you did not intend it to go, he or she *is not* the *right* older person. You also need to observe what is happening in the older person's life—are they going from one drama to the next, or are they living a fairly peaceful and comfortable existence?

There are two types of *right* older people:

- Those who have made mistakes and bad decisions, acquired wisdom and knowledge through the school of hard knocks, and *don't* want you to follow in their footsteps. They will do their best to talk you out of doing something you will regret later. They may point to themselves as an example of why you shouldn't do something you're thinking about doing, or shouldn't continue on the path you're currently taking.
- Those who are successful (by which I mean they have been able to support themselves and any family they have; they have done things to make their community a better place; and they have been able to do some of the things they enjoy in life). These older people have wisdom and knowledge that can help younger people *avoid* some of life's pitfalls:
  - They have been there and done that, or seen the impact on someone else's life that being there and doing that had. As a consequence, they know how to steer clear of bumps in the road.
  - They have overcome obstacles thrown in their way by those who want to prevent them from achieving their goals. Therefore, they can provide information and ideas about overcoming obstacles.
  - They have dealt with disappointment and loss, turned these potential defeats into victories, and moved on with their lives. So, they can share techniques for mending a broken heart *before* it becomes a broken spirit that can dash all dreams and hope for the future—turning a promising life into an empty one.
  - They have dealt with difficult people in a way that has neutralized the impact those people have on their lives, and have done so in a way that did not derail their life's plan.
  - They have figured out how to stretch their dollars so they can live comfortably today *and* in their old age. In short, they have gained enough wisdom to live a full and productive life.

So, don't automatically dismiss what someone says because of their age. Look at how their lives are going, and connect with those who are *not* living in a state of constant drama.

Older people are not irrelevant. In fact, their advice and their example may provide a road map that will help you get where *you* want to be in life more quickly and directly.

History is a Guide for the Future

I love history. I didn't always feel this way. All the way through high school I thought history was just about memorizing dates and reading about the same people and events over and over again. When I got to Syracuse University, however, I took a class entitled *The Social and Cultural History of the United States*, and my attitude changed completely. The professor, Nelson Blake, brought history to life and made it relevant not only through the enthusiastic way he taught the class, but also by his approach to history.

Through his book, *A History of American Life and Thought*, I learned that history is really what people create as they live their lives, develop ideas, take actions in response to the world in which they live, and seek ways to improve their situation. I also learned that history impacts culture by changing the conditions that people live in. For example, when I went to college, a computer was something that filled an entire room. Only those who could learn and understand programming code were able to use a computer. Now I write on a computer that fits on my desk, and on a laptop I can carry with me wherever I go. With just a few keystrokes and the click of a button I have access to knowledge, information and people all over the world. I also use a hand-held computer to keep track of my schedule.

I also learned four other things in Professor Blake's class:

1. **In a very broad sense, all human beings (regardless of their nationality, race or ethnicity) have had common goals and experiences throughout history:**
   - The need to provide adequate food, clothing and shelter for themselves and their families.
   - The desire for order and safety in their lives.
   - The drive to develop innovations that improve daily life.
   - The desire for equal opportunity and access to a better life.
   - The need for creative expression.
   - The need to cope with natural and manmade challenges and disasters.
   - Periods of conflict and war.

2. **The past provides you lessons about what works and what doesn't work:**
   - If you don't give people a fair and equal chance in life, they will rebel.
   - If you don't treat people with respect, you will not get it.
   - If you try to cheat someone, you will pay the price for your dishonesty.
   - If you want to get ahead in life, you have to prepare yourself.
   - If you want something in life, you must be willing to work for it.
   - If you want something to change, you have to take action to make change happen.

3. **History is a guide for the future.** It can teach you how to move from where you are to where you want to be. History teaches how individuals achieved success against tremendous odds, defying predictions they would never do anything worthwhile. Applying their life lessons to your life can help you overcome challenges, positively impact your self-image, and shape your belief about what you can accomplish.

4. **How actions and discoveries can change the course of human life.**
   - How the creation of new technology can make people's lives easier (for example: indoor plumbing,

central heating and air conditioning, electric lights, telephones, mass transportation, computers).

- How powerful ideas can change the lives of many people for the better (for example: public education, equality, nonviolence, human rights, freedom of religion).
- How groups of people working together can change the balance of power between the haves and the have nots (for example: the civil rights movement, the labor movement, women's push for the right to vote, the movement to ensure food safety, the movement to ensure safety in the workplace).

Who we are today, what our lives are like, and the culture in which we live are all linked to history—what happened in the past. But this does not mean we have to be stuck with what we have—that we can't change the present or shape the future. If we learn about and from history, we can improve our lives and avoid making the same mistakes that were made in the past—mistakes that delayed or derailed human progress. Through knowledge and understanding of history we can lay the groundwork for a brighter future for ourselves and those who come after us; and find motivation to take actions that create positive change in our lives, our communities and our world.

DECISIONS HAVE CONSEQUENCES

Life is a series of choices. The decisions you make determine the next set of choices you have to pick from. If you choose to stay in school, learn as much as you can, and go on to college or some other training that will lead to a family-supporting job, you have one set of choices that leads to one lifestyle. If you decide to do the opposite, you end up with another set of choices that lead to another lifestyle. This is not to say that if you make a wrong choice your life is doomed. It's just that getting things turned around when you make bad choices will likely require extra time and effort just to get you back on the road to achieving your dreams.

The decision to not finish high school, for example, can be economic suicide. The 2000 Census found that a high school dropout earned an average of $19,576 per year, compared to $25,244 for high school graduates, $32,985 for those with an associate degree, $43,305 for people with a college degree, and $52,537 for those with a master's degree.

That's only the tip of the iceberg. A 2006 report produced for the Bill & Melinda Gates Foundation found a person who drops out of high school before graduating is:

- 72% more likely to be unemployed.
- More likely to go to jail. (75% of state prisoners and 59% of federal prisoners are high school dropouts).

I saw a news story about the growing number of young people who are dropping out of high school. They interviewed a young man who decided to drop out of school at 18. Perhaps out of boredom, he decided to commit a crime. When they interviewed him from his jail cell, he said he thought he was grown because he was 18, but said he wished he had stayed in school.

The decision not to learn as much as you can while you're in school can also have a negative impact on your future. For example, it can affect whether and where you can go for more education and training after high school. In today's world, even if you don't plan to go to a four-year college or university, you have to go somewhere to get additional training if you want to get a job that pays a living wage. The days of dropping out of school and getting a good-paying factory job are gone. Your competition for jobs is people from all over the world. In places like China, India, and Ireland, high educational performance is expected and pushed. That's why a lot of jobs like data entry, customer service, and some parts of health care are done by people overseas. If you're not academically prepared when you leave high school, you'll have to work twice as hard to catch up on learning education basics at the same time you're trying to learn new skills that can land you a good-paying job.

The decision to let something someone says or does draw you into a fight can also send your life off in a direction you didn't intend for it to go. In a society that is increasingly intolerant of violence, young people who in the past might have been suspended from school for fighting are now being charged with crimes that put them in the criminal justice system. Being part of that system often turns into a slippery slope that leads to deeper and more entangled connections with that system.

Teen pregnancy also is a slippery slope. According to a 2007 U.S. Department of Agriculture report, the cost to a single parent of raising *one* child from birth to age 17 is $140,520. That number doesn't include paying for major illnesses or other unexpected expenses. Since teen mothers are more likely to drop out of school, they end up with lower-paying jobs. The result: more teen moms and their children live in poverty. In a society where the social safety net (welfare) has been all but removed, a teen mom in a low-wage job would have a hard time coming up with $140,520. There certainly are examples of young mothers who beat the odds and not only survived, but successfully raised their children. But for four out of five teen moms, that is not the case.

The long and short of what I'm saying is everything you do in life has consequences. That's why it's important to think things through before you act. Even when you think things through you may make a mistake. It's part of being human. But thinking things through reduces the likelihood that those mistakes will be life changing in a negative way.

Don't become paralyzed trying to avoid mistakes. Life does not stand still. It keeps moving. If *you don't* decide how you want your life to be, you open yourself up to the very real possibility that someone else who doesn't necessarily have your best interest in mind will decide what happens to you. No decision is, in reality, a decision to turn your life over to chance, and chance is a cruel master.

To maintain *some* control over my life and minimize the number and impact of the mistakes I make, I've found it helpful to have ideas about what I want my life to be like in five years. Having a goal in mind helps me pause *before* I do something to consider whether my actions will help or hurt my chances of getting where I want to be. This pause increases the likelihood I'll make the right decision. Snap decisions aren't always the best decisions—especially if someone is trying to talk you into doing something that may be risky or illegal. The best way to reduce the number of snap decisions you might feel compelled to make is to:

- **Have a plan for getting where you want to go:**
  - Decide what your ultimate life goal is. Be as specific as possible. Don't just say "I want to be rich." Think about what kind of work you want to do; do you want a job or do you want to own your own business. Along the way you may change your mind, but having a goal gives your life direction.
  - Determine what you need to do to reach your ultimate goal (education/training, equipment/tools, money, etc.).
  - Identify people who can help you reach your ultimate goal. (You should always evaluate the advice people give you based on whether it will take you toward or away from your goal, and whether the ideas they share with you are in line with your values—what you consider right and ethical.)

- **Put the plan in writing; it will help keep you on task.**
  - ° Divide the plan into shorter time periods with specific things you need to accomplish to keep moving toward your goal. Dividing your plan into bite-sized pieces allows you to see progress.
  - ° Check steps off as you complete them. Seeing signs of progress help keep you encouraged, and working to reach your goal.

Taking this approach will help you reduce the number of detours you take and speed bumps you hit on your journey through life.

BEING GROWN

According to the laws in the United States you're an adult once you turn 18-years-old. But there's a lot more to being grown than reaching a certain age. Based on definitions from the Merriam-Webster Dictionary, there are people in their 20s, 30s, 40s, 50s, 60s and up who still aren't adults. The dictionary defines an adult as someone who is "fully developed and mature; not childish or immature." One of the dictionary's definitions of childish is "one strongly influenced by another or by a place or state of affairs." Childish people:

- **Often act on impulse rather than think things through.** They do whatever crosses their mind without giving it much thought. Adults recognize actions have consequences and think about the impact of their actions *before* they act.

- **Blame others for things that go wrong in their lives—even if it is their behavior or actions that created the problem.** Adults take responsibility for their actions, do what they can to correct mistakes, and pay for any damage they have done.

- **Focus primarily on themselves, and care little about what happens to others.** What matters most to childish people is *their* happiness. As long as they're happy, it doesn't matter how others feel. Adults care about themselves *and* others. They try to treat others the way they would like to be treated, and do what they can to make a positive difference in other people's lives.

- **Depend on others to take care of them.** Adults know *they* are responsible for their own well being, and do everything they can to take care of themselves.

- **Go along to get along.** Childish people follow the crowd, even if the crowd is going down a path that is destructive for themselves and for others. Adults think for themselves and try to make good decisions that will lead to a better life, rather than to a more difficult one.

- **Focus on the here and now.** Childish people seldom think about where they want to be in the future and what they need to do to get there. Adults think about what they want their lives to be like, commit to getting the training and education they need, and are willing to work and make sacrifices to succeed.

While it may seem like more fun to be a child, ultimately you don't have a choice about whether you can act like a child or an adult. As you get older, people are less willing to give you a pass when you do something childish. They may laugh about something you did when you were small, but if you do the same things when you're an adult they may call the police, take you to court, make you pay a fine, or put you in jail because you're "old enough to know better."

The people you hang out with have a big influence on whether you act like a child or like an adult. If you hang out with childish people who have no direction in their lives, and focus on having a good time, you likely won't have any direction in your life. If you hang out with people who are fully developed and mature, it's more likely you will be also.

Don't be fooled into thinking you're an adult by buying into the definition based strictly on age. Being an adult is much more complex than that. Not recognizing this complexity can lead to bad decisions that can take much if not all of your life to correct.

CHILDHOOD IS NOT FOREVER

In high school one of my classmates made it her mission to make my life miserable. My crime? I was a good student. Whenever she saw me, my classmate would do something to intimidate me or try to make me feel bad. She might bump me in the hall, say something negative about me as we passed in the hallway, or stare at me like she'd like to rip my heart out. I did my best to avoid her in school; but I didn't let her behavior stop me from getting good grades. I graduated third in my class.

Years later—after I had graduated from college, gotten my master's degree, become an award-winning newspaper reporter, and moved back to Milwaukee where I worked in marketing for a major corporation—I ran into my former classmate. I didn't notice her at first, but she saw me. She called my name. When I turned around and saw her, my armpits broke out in sweat. More than 10 years after I had last seen her, she still struck fear in me.

Since I couldn't pretend I didn't see her, I braced myself for whatever negative thing she was going to do, and walked toward her. To my surprise, she didn't start in on me. She asked me what I had been doing since I graduated from high school. I told her. She said I obviously was having a good life. I asked about her life. The story was not positive. She had married, had a family and was divorced. She was working, but her job didn't pay enough for her and her children to live on. Then she said something that really surprised me: she admitted she had done her best to make my life miserable in high school, and said she wished she had applied herself academically the way I did. Had she done so, she said, she and her family wouldn't be struggling.

My former classmate was one of the most popular girls in high school. I must admit I sometimes wished I could be popular like her. But I was shy. She was also very smart but, as she said, she didn't focus on learning.

I tried to encourage her, and though I didn't say so, I felt sad for her. I have not seen her since that encounter. The last I heard she was living in Texas. I hope she has been able to turn things around in her life.

My conversation with my former classmate helped me realize several things:

- One of the differences between being a child and being an adult is that someone else *might* clean up your mess when you make a mistake as a child. But when you become an adult, you can't act on impulse all the time and expect other people to take care of the consequences. Adults think about what they're doing and its impact on themselves and others.
- While we think we'll be young forever, the truth is we get older every day. Before we know it, we're responsible for taking care of ourselves and, perhaps, others. Therefore, it's important to be prepared for those responsibilities.
- Decisions you make when you're young can have a long term impact on your future. While bad decisions don't have to be permanent, they can make getting your life in order a lot harder.

As much as we would like to remain kids forever, it's not going to happen. We *can and should* maintain the enthusiasm, excitement, curiosity, and "can do" attitude that we have as children. Being an adult is not all drudgery and work and seriousness. We don't have to be grumpy and never have fun. In fact, we should have fun! But we also have to recognize that childhood—living our lives as though we have no responsibility for our actions and no responsibility to anybody but ourselves—does not last forever.

All That, and a Bag of Chips

Popular culture likes to shine the spotlight on those who are rich, powerful, or famous. The culture would have you believe we all should aspire to be like those in the spotlight.

While there certainly is nothing wrong with being rich, powerful or famous, those qualities alone are not the standard by which people who make a lasting difference in life are measured. You see proof of this when those who buy into the hype and act as though the rules that apply to everyone else don't apply to them fall from grace. On any given day you can read or hear about:

- Athletes involved in gambling, gunplay, drug use, or inappropriate personal behavior.
- Business people who misused corporate funds, didn't pay taxes, or sold products they knew where harmful.
- Elected officials who accepted bribes, engaged in extortion or otherwise violated their public trust.
- Entertainers who abuse alcohol, drugs or make inappropriate statements.
- Clergy who engage in misconduct or misuse funds.

When things like this happen, public opinion is quick to change. Instead of being someone people look up to, these individuals become subject to gossip and ridicule. The respect they once had disappears. The "friends" they once thought they had—the ones who came along for the ride while they were on top—go away. For athletes and entertainers, the fall from grace often hits them hard in the pocketbook when advertisers and sponsors drop them like a hot rock.

What those who fall from their pedestal fail to remember is *nobody* is all that. We are all sinners saved by grace. If we want to truly make our mark in life—to be remembered, appreciated, and thought of as a great person—we must remain humble. By that I don't mean we have to put ourselves down. Rather, we should recognize we are not the Second Coming.

My father, Mack Payton, was a humble man. He worked hard, took care of his family, and did what he could to help other people. As a juvenile probation officer (and later probation officer supervisor), he came in contact with young people whose lives were heading in the wrong direction. He helped steer many of them in the right direction. When dad died, one of those young men talked about how my father had helped turn his life around. That troubled young man grew up to become . . . a probation officer.

My mother, Gertrude, is a retired home economics teacher and guidance counselor. I frequently run into people she had as students—some of whom are older than me—who talk about the positive impact "Miss Payton" had on their lives.

Neither of my parents sought special recognition or the spotlight, but many people know them, know of them and respect them. If you're really all that, you don't have to tell people about it. They know it. If you wear your achievements with quiet grace, they'll be there for you when you need them. When dad died, people not only came out of the woodwork to show up for his funeral and say nice things about him, but they continued to be there for the family months after the funeral was over. The *Milwaukee Journal Sentinel* newspaper thought the story of his life was worth putting in the paper. Many people contributed money to a family fund we established during my father's lifetime to help others. His alma mater, Alcorn State University, where he and my mother set up a scholarship fund, paid special tribute to him. And citations from local, county, state and federal officials were issued in honor of his life.

Not bad for a humble, quiet man who didn't act like he was all that and a bag of chips.

You Won't Succeed at Everything You Try, But You Will Learn Something From Everything You Do

We are a nation of score keepers. Whether it's in sports, politics, business, the arts or other areas of life, we like to focus on winners and losers. In politics, media coverage of campaigns is not so much about what people stand for as it is about how much money candidates have raised, how many people showed up for a rally, how many endorsements candidates received. If a person is not the front runner, the assumption is he or she cannot win.

In business the news coverage (even in local media) is usually about the biggest companies making the most money rather than the small firms that collectively employ most of the people in this country, and are the engine that drives the economy.

In the arts the focus is often on who is an "A list" celebrity rather than on who is producing works of substance and quality.

Even in our daily lives there is a tendency to keep score. Many measure their success by how their lifestyle—material possessions, ability to be in the mix, etc.—stacks up against someone else's. If they don't have what someone else has, they feel they're missing out. Success, in this context, is defined as who has the most money, the most things, the most power, the most prestigious list of friends and associates.

What is lost in this score-card approach to viewing the world is that life is not just about winning and losing. Life, lived right, is a journey that leads to growth, development and improvement. You learn not only from those things that you do right and do well, but also from those things that don't go well. Scientist know this very well. Whether they are looking for a cure for a disease or they're trying to determine how to reduce global warming, developing new devices to make day-to-day life more comfortable and easy to manage, or trying to find new ways to grow food to reduce hunger, scientists know it will take more than one try to reach their goal. When something does not work, instead of ignoring the "failure," they analyze what they did to find out what changes they need to make to get back on track. Often their research and development takes years to complete, but they don't give up.

This approach, to me, is a model to follow as we live our lives. We won't succeed at everything we try—especially on the first try. But if we don't give up, if we analyze what happened when things don't go as expected to see what changes we need to make to get back on track, if we learn from our setbacks so we won't repeat the same mistakes, then we will be on the road that leads to a better, more fulfilling, productive and satisfying life.

The Most Important Thing You Have is Your Good Name

The most important thing you have is your good name. Once you lose that, it is difficult to regain it. This can impact your future in negative ways. Therefore, it is important to do everything possible to earn and keep your good name:

Be a person of your word. If you say you're going to do something, do it. If something comes up that prevents you from doing what you said, let someone know as soon as possible. People like to deal with those they can depend on. Once you develop a reputation for being a person of your word, you'd be amazed at the opportunities that will come your way.

Don't give references for people unless you know they will live up to what you say about them; and don't allow anyone to use your name as a reference without your permission. This is another aspect of being dependable. When you develop a reputation for giving people an honest assessment of a person's ability to do a job or complete a project, people will know they can trust your referrals. They will give anyone you recommend serious consideration for whatever opportunities they have.

Don't gossip about other people. Most people think if you talk about other people behind their backs, you will also talk about them.

Therefore, they are less likely to trust you. Also, you don't always know to whom you're talking. You may assume you're talking to someone who has no relationship to the person you're talking about, and the next thing you know, word has gotten back to the person you were talking about. That sort of gossip can kill a relationship with someone who could help you reach some of your goals, or open up opportunities for you.

If you make a mistake, admit it and do what you can to correct it. We all make mistakes. Many people try to cover up their mistakes rather than admit them. Frequently they discover the penalty for a cover-up is worse than the penalty for the offense itself. In some instances a cover-up could get you kicked out of school or fired from your job; in other instances it could lead to criminal charges. A number of high-profile politicians, business people and athletes have gone to jail or paid huge fines not because of what they did, but because they tried to cover up the truth.

Don't hesitate to say you're sorry *and mean it.* Like admitting a mistake, saying you're sorry and meaning it helps people trust you. Most people are willing to forgive if you say you're sorry. They tend not to trust you (and may harbor resentment against you) if you don't. Again, creating this lack of trust could have a negative impact on your ability to achieve your goals in life.

Be honest Don't exaggerate your school or work background to impress someone. Don't try to make yourself appear more important and accomplished than you really are. The truth will always come out. When it does, it will negatively impact your ability to get what you want out of life.

Having your good name is the first step on the road to achieving your dreams.

ACHIEVING SUCCESS

Everything You're Looking for
is Not Straight Ahead of You

Sometimes what we're looking for in life is right there, but we miss it because we only look straight in front of us instead of looking all around to see what we can see.

An incident that happened while I was visiting the Descanso Gardens in Pasadena, CA with family members is an example of what I'm talking about. One of my relatives needed to go to the bathroom. I pointed in the direction of the restroom sign and said, "It's over there." A minute later I decided making a pit stop of my own might not be a bad idea before beginning the 45-minute walking tour, so I also headed to the bathroom. No one was there but me. Thirty seconds later, my relative arrived. As we left, I asked her how I had arrived before her. She said "I walked straight ahead and didn't look to the left or right." Because the bathroom was on the left, she had to circle back and begin her search again.

Just like my relative missed the bathroom by not looking around, it's easy to miss life's opportunities, obstacles and (worse case scenario) threats if you don't pay attention to what's going on around you. I believe popular culture has contributed to this tendency to miss what's happening around us because pop culture spends more time focusing on the end results—success—than on telling the back story about how much time and effort it took a person or group to prepare to reach their goal. You seldom hear about the small steps and detours someone had to make to get where he or she is. You almost never see how many times people tried and failed—fell down and got up—on their way to the place they wanted to be in life. You seldom hear about the people who intentionally or by accident tried to discourage someone from pursuing what *they* considered to be a "foolish dream," and how hard it was for the "dreamer" to keep the faith and push on. You seldom hear about those who opened doors or provided encouragement along the way. All you see is the result. Because popular culture often doesn't deal with the big picture of success (the ups and downs, barriers and detours, successes *and* failures) people are less likely to understand how complex achieving your life goals is. More times than not, success requires you to make adjustments to:

- Your plan (what you're going to do to get where you want to go).
- Your timeline (when you do something that moves you toward your goal, or when you think you'll achieve your goal).
- Your goal (what it is you want to achieve).

This last point—adjustments to your goal—is particularly important. I don't mean you should jump from one goal to another. It *is* important to be focused. If you're not, you could go through life without *finishing* anything. But sometimes people are so fixated on following a particular path that they won't take advantage of other opportunities that could get them where they want to go faster or lead them to an even better destination. They may decide not to take a job out of town because they don't want to leave the comfortable, familiar surroundings of family and friends—even if the new job would move them closer to achieving their life goals. Sometimes people are afraid to try new career or volunteer opportunities because those opportunities are in a field in which they have little or no prior experience. Yet, those opportunities could open doors to a life they might never have thought about before.

I remember running into a high school classmate when I moved back to Milwaukee to take a new job. He was working for a mayoral candidate and asked me to help out. The volunteer work didn't involve a lot of heavy lifting, just providing advice and introductions to people I knew in the community. I had never done anything like this before, but agreed to do so as a favor.

When the candidate won, I was asked to serve on the Metropolitan Milwaukee Sewerage District Commission, which is responsible for overseeing the planning and operation of the waste water treatment facility that serves 28 municipalities within Milwaukee County and parts of surrounding counties. At first I was reluctant because I didn't know anything about sewers other than the fact they were in the ground and when I flushed it worked.

When I made that comment, the response I got from the new mayor was "You're smart. You can figure it out." I agreed, and accepted the opportunity. I was elected chair of the Commission, which at the time was overseeing a $2.1 billion deep tunnel construction project. That experience helped me develop and sharpen my management and budget skills, and make connections with political and business leaders in the metropolitan area that I would not otherwise have made. While I don't pal around with these individuals, I am comfortable interacting with people at that level.

Accepting the opportunity also allowed me to increase the number of firms owned by people of color and women that did business with the District, and to spearhead hiring the first African American to head the District's day-to-day operations by expanding the outlets used to get the word out about the job opening. Had we not expanded our outreach he might never have known about the job, and we might never have known about him. When all the resumes were in, he was the consensus number one candidate based on qualifications alone.

There are many examples of unforeseen opportunities that lead to unforeseen changes in our lives and in history. While I am certainly *not* putting myself in the same category as Dr. Martin Luther King, Jr., his decision to detour from his original life plan shows, on a much greater scale than any decision I've made, what can happen.

Dr. King's original dream was to pastor a large church like his father. After Rosa Parks refused to give up her seat and was arrested, Dr. King was approached to lead a boycott of the segregated Montgomery bus system. Though a young man, he accepted the challenge. Because he took a detour, Dr. King's impact on human life is much greater than it might have been had he stayed with his original plan. People in such places as Prague, Czechoslovakia, India, South Africa and elsewhere have been inspired by Dr. King's actions and message to use non-violence to achieve justice and equality in their countries.

So, as you go through life, remember that the best opportunities are not always straight ahead of you. When a new opportunity comes along, think about it, pray about it, analyze the opportunity to determine whether it will take you closer to or away from you original goal. If it takes you away from your original goal, ask yourself whether the place it's leading you to is better or worse in terms of its impact on your life and the lives of others. Once you've done this and determined that the opportunity is something you'd like to pursue, don't be afraid to move in that new direction. It could lead you to a more satisfying and productive life than you ever thought possible.

A Better Life, A Better
World Starts With Vision

I was in high school during the "Camelot" days when the Kennedys were in the White House and the country was full of optimism and hope. I think what made those days so upbeat was that both President John F. Kennedy and his brother Robert, the U.S. Attorney General, were visionaries who were able to communicate their vision to the rest of the country.

A little over a year after his election, President Kennedy announced that the United States would land a man on the moon and return him safely home by the end of the decade. The announcement was made in response to the Soviet Union's launch of the *Sputnik 1* satellite into space—an event that sent shock waves through the United States because, at the time, the Soviet Union was America's Cold War enemy. (The Cold War was a political and economic struggle for supremacy after World War II between two systems of government—communism, whose lead champion was the Soviet Union and democracy whose lead champion was the United States. Both the Soviet Union and the United States considered supremacy in space exploration important to their national security and a way to demonstrate the superiority of their technology and system of government. One of America's fears was that the Soviet Union would colonize the moon and be able to launch attacks on the United States from that location.)

President Kennedy's announcement electrified the country. Schools began to ramp up teaching math and science. Scientists and engineers began to work on identifying what it would take to achieve that goal. While President Kennedy did not live to see it happen, the U.S. did, in fact, land men on the moon and returned them safely to earth.

During his own presidential campaign in 1968 then-Sen. Robert Kennedy, paraphrasing Irish playwright George Bernard Shaw, said "There are those who look at things the way they are, and ask why . . . I dream of things that never were, and ask why not?" This quote, to me, summarizes how each of us can make a difference in our own lives and the lives of others. Just because things are the way they are doesn't mean they have to stay that way. If you are willing to ask why something can't be different, willing to think about what you can do to make things different, and willing to *act* to make things different, then you can improve your life circumstances as well as the lives of others. No matter what your situation in life is, if you're willing to dream about a better life, and work to make that dream a reality, things can and will get better.

If you only accept what is, things will not change. It's what psychologists call the self-fulfilling prophecy—if you believe something is true, you will act as though it's true, and it will become true. If litter and trash are being thrown on the ground in your neighborhood and nobody picks it up, the problem of litter and trash will get worse. If conflict and violence occurs in your school or community and no one does anything to stop it, it will not only continue but get worse. If poor educational achievement occurs in schools and no one does anything to improve educational outcomes, things will get worse. If unemployment is growing in a community and nobody does anything to create jobs and to make sure people have the education and training to do those jobs, unemployment will get worse.

Envisioning positive change and taking steps to make that vision a reality will *not* make everything better immediately. But like a minor earthquake just below the ocean's floor can produce a large, powerful wave, even small changes can make a big difference over time. Mothers Against Drunk Driving—an organization committed to reducing traffic deaths due to drunk drivers—began as a small act by a mother whose child was killed in such an accident. The end of legal segregation began with acts of civil disobedience in cities and towns (such as the Montgomery Bus Boycott and sit-ins at lunch counters that would not serve food to Black people).

So even when a situation *seems* like it will never change, don't assume this is true. Create a vision in your mind about what a better life and a better world would look like, and then take steps to make that vision come true.

The Strongest Part of Your Body is Your Brain

You wouldn't know it by watching television, movies, music videos, or listening to music, but the strongest part of your body is your brain. Intelligence is not given the same play as beauty, celebrity or athletic ability. We don't hold pep rallies in schools for the debate team or chess team. Most students don't get letter sweaters for academic achievement. We don't hold parades for prize-winning poets, authors, artists, composers, or scientists. Yet the world we live in today runs on brainpower. We live in an information age. The jobs available to most people will be connected to information development, use, storage, distribution, sharing and support. That means the ones who will have the best jobs and run the world are those who know how to develop, use or control information. Don't believe me? Some of the world's richest people made money using their brains:

- Microsoft founder Bill Gates used his brain to makes billions of dollars by developing computer software.
- Investment tycoon Warren Buffett—known by those who follow his investment advice as the "Oracle of Omaha"—used his brain to make $10 billion in one year.
- Oprah Winfrey used her brain to build her multi-billion dollar communication empire.

- B. Smith used her brain to establish a successful chain of restaurants, develop a jewelry and home décor product line, and author lifestyle books.
- American Girl creator Pleasant Rowland used her brain to make millions of dollars by creating a doll, book and accessories empire based on stories from the viewpoint of girls living at various times in American history.
- Bob Johnson used his brain to found Black Entertainment Television (BET), which helped make him a billionaire.
- Businessman and publisher John Johnson, who founded Johnson Publishing Company (publisher of *Ebony* and *Jet* magazines), was the first African American to appear on *Forbes* magazine's list of the top 400 richest Americans. He made his money using his brain.

The success of these business people who used brainpower emanates from the fact that human brains are the world's greatest super computer. Human brains can help you:

- Solve problems.
- Come up with new ideas.
- Identify ways to make those ideas work.
- Out-think competitors.

Those who can do these things well will be in high demand in the job market for years to come, and will have great opportunities for starting and growing successful businesses. Everyone won't become ridiculously wealthy, but brain power is the most certain road to living a comfortable, enjoyable and productive life.

A television news story about improvements in job opportunities for recent college graduates said those opportunities were in the high tech field. Graduates were being offered serious money and other benefits by technology companies who need qualified workers. These opportunities are occurring during one of the worse economic periods since the Great Depression.

While most people think of brainpower as something only computer geeks need, those who work with their hands also have to use brainpower. Carpenters, plumbers, electricians, iron workers, auto mechanics, and heavy equipment operators (among others) need to have more than strong backs to do their jobs. The equipment they work with requires them to understand such things as geometry, physics, and electronics.

The superiority of brain power is not a new thing. Throughout history (even before the information age began) there are many examples that prove brainpower is more powerful than physical power:

- In the story of David and Goliath, David thought through what he needed to do to defeat the giant Goliath. Goliath's plan was the usual: physically overpower his opponent and squash him like a bug. David's strategy was not to let Goliath get close enough to touch him. Knowing that he was accurate with a slingshot and stones, David decided to use this "technology" to stop Goliath in his tracks. He used his sling shot to hit Goliath in the head with a stone, and Goliath was killed instantly.
- Harriet Tubman, a small woman, used her brains to outfox slave catchers and lead hundreds of people to freedom.
- Mahatma Ghandi and Martin Luther King Jr. used the power of an idea (non-violence) to help liberate oppressed people in India and America.

Brainpower is also important in your personal life. Being able to think things through before you act can prevent problems and keep you out of trouble. I believe if people paused before they spoke and thought about how they could resolve an issue they have with someone before snapping on them, a lot of arguments, hurt feelings, fights and injuries could be avoided. If more people spent more time thinking about what they really want in life and put together and implemented a plan to get there, they'd increase their chances for success and enjoyment.

There is a reason we human beings (unlike other animals) have brains with the ability to reason. If we use our brains well, we can lead a satisfying life and leave the world a better place for those who follow us.

EDUCATION IS A LIFE-LONG PROCESS

Even if you lived to be 300 years old, you could never know all there is to know. Not only is there a lot from the past to learn about, but new information, ideas and inventions develop almost daily. That's why I consider education a life-long process.

Each day gives you a chance to learn something new. You can learn:

- How the world around you works.
- About other people, other cultures, other ideas.
- About yourself—what you do best, what you like and don't like, what you want most in life.

Using your mind to learn new things, reflect on what's going on in your life, and identify what you can do to improve yourself helps keep you young and mentally sharp. As doctors will tell you, it's as important to exercise your mind as it is to exercise your body if you want to stay in shape throughout your life. In addition, continuous learning gives you a reason to get up in the morning because you realize every day is different from the day before, and offers opportunities you've never had before. What you learn helps you see life from different perspectives (which makes life more interesting), and helps you take a more positive approach to living.

Education is not just something that takes place in school. You can learn:

- By watching people and listening to what they say.
- By reading books, newspapers and magazines.
- By talking to or reading about people who have achieved what you want to achieve.
- By going to museums, traveling to places you haven't been before (including places in your home town like museums, cultural events, programs at local colleges), learning new skills, taking classes in art, music, dance, theatre, business, science and technology, foreign language, history, carpentry, photography, plumbing, etc.
- By playing sports.
- By sitting and watching nature—how clouds form and move, how ants work together, how birds fly in formation, how water moves things around, how the sun rises and sets differently, how the wind can blow things around in different ways.
- From the past as well as the present. It's been said there is nothing new under the sun. I've lived long enough to believe that's true. Some of the attitudes and behavior I see in the world and this country today are very similar to things I remember as a child. I recently completed a play set in 1859—two years before the U.S. Civil War began. Many of the attitudes and concerns back then exist in 2011, and for many of the same reasons: a sharp economic downturn, fear of loss of power, fear of change. Knowing the past and the results that attitudes and behaviors produced back then can help us avoid making the same mistakes in today's world.

Continuous learning is important. Whatever you learn, no one can take away from you. Knowledge is power. It gives you information to use when you're trying to decide what to do or not do. Having more knowledge also helps you see life as more manageable. While you can't be in absolute control of everything that happens, you can have some impact on how things turn out by using the information you have to benefit yourself and others.

It's been said that an idle mind is the devil's workshop. I think that's because the mind is always looking for something to do. If you don't give it something positive to explore, it will find something negative to do, leading to decisions you may regret later.

So keep learning as long as you're inhaling air. It will make your life richer not only in material ways, but also in terms of personal enjoyment and satisfaction.

IF YOU DON'T KNOW, PEOPLE
CAN TELL YOU ANYTHING

One of the things I learned as a reporter for the *Miami Herald* was the importance of checking your sources. People can tell you anything, and say it with such authority that you are convinced they are absolutely right even though they are absolutely wrong. That is why, as a reporter, I always got information from multiple sources and looked for written sources of information against which to check my facts.

There are a number of reasons people say things that are not true. The most common is that they just get their facts mixed up. Others will make things up because they don't want to admit they don't know the answer. Some may want to impress you with their knowledge. Some think they're doing you a favor by giving you an answer whether it's correct or not.

When something that can impact your life is on the line—decisions about education and career, situations with legal implications, things involving money and finance, health, and retirement—it's important to get the facts for yourself. Don't take someone's word for it. With internet access it is relatively easy to gather information on just about any subject. Of course you need to make sure the site you visit is reliable. There are a lot of sites where people express their opinions, which may or may not coincide with the facts. Sites that end in .edu, .org or .gov are generally more reliable.

Also, don't limit yourself to the internet. Look up things in books and data bases at the library, talk to people who are knowledgeable about the subject. When making a career decision, either volunteer or try to get a job in the field you are considering before you make a final decision so you can observe what really goes on on the job.

If you don't know, people can tell you anything. That's why it's important to make sure you've done your homework and *know* that you know, not *think* that you know. Knowledge is power and can keep you from making serious mistakes that could set you back or derail your dreams.

IF YOU DON'T KNOW YOUR STORY, OTHERS CAN DEFINE WHO YOU ARE

I've noticed most people aren't interested in history. They're more focused on the here and now than on what happened in the past. Certainly it is important to pay attention to what's going on now, to think about what you want to happen in the future, and to determine what you need to do to achieve your goals. But I also believe it is important to know history.

Spanish-American philosopher, poet, essayist and novelist George Santayana once said, "Those who cannot remember the past are condemned to repeat it." I believe this not only applies to history in its broadest sense, but also to history in a personal sense—the history and culture of the people from whom you are descended. Knowing that history and culture reminds you that you are standing on the shoulders of those who came before you, and helps you appreciate the things they did to help you get where you are today. This history ties you to traditions that can be a source of strength and pride, and can serve as a touchstone for making decisions about what to do and what not to do. This history can help you find common ground with those within your cultural group *and* identify similar (if not identical) traditions in other cultural groups that can serve as the basis for cooperation and understanding across racial, cultural and ethnic lines. This history can be a shield against forces that would try to tear down your sense of self-worth by showing you that *all* cultural groups have made positive contributions to human history.

If you don't know your story—the history of the people from whom you are descended—then someone else can make up stories about who you are based on their stereotype of the racial, cultural or ethnic group you belong to. What they tell you may not be true, but if you don't know better, their reality can become your reality, which can influence what you think about yourself and the options you have in life (both of which impact how you live your life).

The life you live based on *someone else's* reality more often than not will *not* be the *best* life you're capable of living.

WHO YOU HANG WITH MATTERS

Several years ago three young men wrote a book entitled *The Pact*. In it they wrote about their lives and how they made a pledge to each other to get out of their tough neighborhood by doing well in high school, going to college and becoming doctors.

They succeeded. All three are doctors: two are medical doctors and one is a dentist. The key to their success, they said, was that they kept each other encouraged *and* in check.

What their story points out is that who you hang out with matter. Those you associate with can influence your behavior for better or for worse. No matter what is going on around you, if you choose to associate with people who are making positive decisions and trying to move forward in a positive direction, your chances of having a productive life are better.

On the other hand, even if you are a positive person and come from a positive and supportive home environment, hanging around people who are not about doing anything productive with their lives, who are always looking for ways to "get over" or game the system, increases the likelihood that your life will include hardships (struggling to get by), jail, or even premature death.

Human beings are social animals. We like to be together. We want those we associate with to like us. That is normal. But you shouldn't have to "prove" anything to be accepted. If those you are hanging with require you to "prove" you're down with them, you're hanging with the wrong crowd.

I had to make a decision when I got to college about whether I would hang with the party crowd or the nerd crowd. I have never been a party animal, but when I got to college I thought I would check things out. During freshman orientation (before classes started) I attended just about every party held at 505 S. Crouse—the hangout place. But when classes began and I realized how academically demanding my schedule was, I stopped partying. My parents were forking out too much money for me not to graduate on time. I focused on what I went to college for—to get a degree. I came out four years later with a double major and 1/10 of a percent shy of graduating with honors. I have not regretted the choice I made. That choice made it possible for me to live a comfortable life and do many of the things I enjoy doing.

As you make choices about who you hang with, remember that these decisions not only affect your life today; they can (and often do) impact the rest of your life.

JEALOUSY

Bertie Charles Forbes, founder of *Forbes Magazine* (one of the top business publications in the country), once said "Jealousy . . . is a mental cancer." That pretty much says it all. Just as cancer eats away at healthy tissues and cells, and (if not stopped) will kill the body, jealousy eats away at your ability to think clearly, and gets in the way of:

- Determining what your goals in life are.
- Determining what you need to reach your life goals.
- Creating and implementing a plan of action for getting where you want to be in life.
- Coming up with solutions to problems that threaten to kill your dreams.

When you're jealous, you spend your time focusing on what *someone else* is doing or has instead of working toward achieving *your* goals. You are so focused on what you *don't* have that you don't recognize what you *do* have and how you can use that to get where you want to be.

Being jealous also makes you unhappy. The frustration and stress that builds up takes a toll on your health and mental well-being. Being stressed or upset can weaken your immune system and (subconsciously) make you neglect your health by not eating properly, exercising, taking prescribed medications unnecessarily, or abusing alcohol or illegal drugs. Poor health can not only make your life more difficult, but also shorten it. In short, jealousy can be so consuming that it can destroy the person who is jealous along with his or her dreams.

Jealousy shows itself in a variety of ways:

- In the up and down look someone gives you when you enter a room in a nice outfit.
- In a sarcastic remark.
- Through bullying, intimidation, and violence.

What makes one person jealous of another? People find all kinds of things to be jealous about. They may:

- Be jealous because another person received recognition and they didn't.
- Be upset about someone else's success because things aren't going well in *their* lives.
- Need to impress others to feel good about themselves.

My parents taught me two things I've used throughout my life to make sure jealousy doesn't prevent me from living the life I dreamed of:

- Focus on my mission—what I want to achieve.
- Get to know and learn from people who are doing something I would like to do or have something I would like to have. They taught me that my chances of getting what I want in life are greater if I *connect* with people who are successful rather than try to undercut them.

I know from experience my parent's advice works. If you want to achieve your dreams, don't let the cancer of jealousy destroy your ability to think clearly, and connect with those who can help you achieve your goals.

Preparation, Hard Work and Determination Beat Luck Every time

When people read or hear the latest news about celebrities, wealthy business people and athletes, they frequently attribute their success to "luck." News flash: luck has little to do with it. Most people who achieve success do so because they had a goal, learned the skills they needed to do the job, worked hard, and never gave up. When you peek behind the curtain and get the full story about how they achieved success and (in some cases) wealth, all of these building blocks are present.

In in-depth interviews about how they made it to the NBA, NFL, Major League Baseball or the Olympics, athletes usually talk about having a dream and putting in hours and hours of time and effort to perfect their skills.

Biographies about millionaire or billionaire business people often contain similar stories about how much time and effort they put into building the enterprises that earned them their millions (and often, how much time and effort they still put into maintaining that enterprise).

In stories about the careers of entertainers who've made millions, their rise to fame and fortune often includes accounts of hard work and perseverance.

It would be nice if carrying a lucky penny, dreaming a number or rubbing a rabbit's foot was all it took to have whatever you want in life. It doesn't work that way.

In a world that is so interconnected that people in other countries will take your catalog order for a pair of shoes or process your bank statement or manufacture the clothes on your back and ship them here for you to wear—depending on "luck" to get what you want out of life makes no sense. Actually, it never did. The first century Roman philosopher Seneca said, "Luck is what happens when preparation meets opportunity." I would add *determination* and *hard work* to Seneca's words.

The inventor Thomas Edison once said, "Opportunity is missed by most people because it's dressed in overalls and looks like work." In other words, whatever you get in life will take preparation, hard work, determination and commitment to get the job done.

"Luck" happens to those who make their own—who find out what it takes to get where they want to go, and dedicate themselves to getting the skills and knowledge needed to *earn* the right to have an opportunity. "Luck" happens to those who put in the time and effort necessary to sharpen their skills to the point that no one can deny their qualifications. "Luck" happens to those who hang on through hard times, disappointment, and times when it seems they aren't being treated fairly; those who, in the words of Rudyard Kipling's poem *If* " . . . hold on when there is nothing in you except the Will which says to them: 'Hold on!' "

If you are willing to prepare yourself to achieve your goals, work hard, and hold on, then "luck" will happen.

HOPE FOR THE BEST AND
PREPARE FOR THE WORST

It would be wonderful if you could live life without experiencing problems. But that's not going to happen. Sometimes the problems that pop up are small. Other times they are pretty significant. You can be sitting in the sunshine enjoying life and suddenly find yourself in the midst of a storm that is threatening to blow all your dreams away. The best way to deal with these storms and to have at least a fighting chance to keep your dreams alive is to hope for the best but prepare for the worst.

My parents taught me not to spend every dime I made, but rather to put money away for a "rainy day." It took an incident in college to really drive that message home. My parents put some money in a bank account for me my freshman year. They told me the money was for my books, other expenses *and* my airfare home for the summer. They said that was all the money they could afford to give me, so I had to spend it wisely.

It was the first time I had been given responsibility to manage my own money, and I almost blew it. Around exam time in my second semester, I realized I had spent so much on "other expenses" (not all of which were necessary) that I didn't have enough to pay for my airfare home. I put signs up on campus offering to type term papers, and was able to make enough money to fly home for the summer. Having gone through that experience, I never came up short again. In fact, when I graduated I had enough money in the bank to pay the first and last month's rent for my first apartment, car insurance and other expenses connected with starting my first job.

When I got my first job I started planning, saving and investing for retirement because I had heard Social Security would not be around when I reached retirement age. While that prediction is not completely true, it's close. Social Security still exists, but the money you get from it is not even close to being what you need to live on. When I changed jobs, I contributed to a retirement account offered by my new employer. When I started my own business, I set up a retirement account for myself; and when I got another job, I contributed to the retirement plan that organization offered. Because I did these things to prepare for the worst, I am able to live comfortably for the rest of my life. It's not the Hollywood version of comfort, but I can take care of my needs and have money left over to do *some* of the things I like to do for fun.

Recently a rainy day literally came along. The roof on my house started to fall apart and, in the middle of a storm, I had rain falling from the ceiling in my spare bedroom. I was semi-retired—working less than 20 hours per week. Fortunately, I hadn't forgotten the lesson I learned years ago about saving for the future. In addition to having some money set aside for retirement, I had some money in a savings account. Between those two sources, I was able to pay for the roof without having to go back to work fulltime. It put a squeeze on me, but it didn't knock me to the ground.

There is no *magic* way to get to this point. Nor is there anything glamorous about it. It's a matter of trying to live within your means (not spend more than you earn), shopping for bargains, and investing rainy day money with the help of a reliable financial adviser who will work with you to make your money earn money at a rate that is higher than the increase in the cost of living.

Knowing I've done what I can to prepare for a rainy day helps take care of one of life's major stresses—paying my bills—and makes it easier to keep hoping for the best.

LEARN SURVIVAL SKILLS

It's wonderful to live in a time when you can pay someone else to do what ever you need done. Whole industries have sprung up to do everything from taking clothes to the dry cleaners to preparing meals to walking the dog to picking up the car and having it serviced or washed to cleaning the house.

As long as you have the money to pay for this help you're set; but there's no guarantee that will be the case. Even so, many of us live our lives based on the assumption things will always be the same: that we will have all the money and other resources we need to maintain our lifestyle. When something happens that negatively impacts our finances, we are not prepared. Any number of things can throw our finances and our lives into a tailspin: an accident or illness, death in the family, loss of a job or retirement benefits (which often means loss of health insurance) a natural disaster like Hurricane Katrina or Irene, or a change in the economy like the sub-prime mortgage collapse that put many people in danger of losing their homes.

Because you can't predict every uncertainty, it is important to have what I call basic survival skills—cooking, sewing, knitting, changing a flat tire, checking and replacing the fluids in your car, doing minor home repairs, being able to grow your own vegetables and preserve them by freezing and canning. It may sound crazy to talk about this in the 21st Century, but all of these skills can help you maintain at least a reasonable quality of life even if your financial situation changes for the worse. Yes, you can eat out or buy pre-cooked foods, but that is more expensive than cooking. Also, the amount of food you get when you eat out often is more than you would normally eat at home; and the way it is prepared often contains more calories, fat and salt than home-cooked meals—all of which could lead to health problems connected with obesity. Yes, you can buy designer clothes, but that is more expensive than shopping at a second-hand or Goodwill store, catching sales, adding personal touches to the clothing you already have or buying accessories that give your existing wardrobe a "new look." And it certainly is more expensive than sewing your own clothes, and mending clothes that have minor rips, tears or missing buttons. Yes, you can call a plumber to stop a leaky faucet, but that is more expensive than learning where to turn the water to the faucet off and how to replace the washer. In tight financial times every penny saved can reduce the stress of paying bills and taking care of day-to-day needs.

You may not use your survival skills on a day-to-day basis, but knowing *how* to do these things can really come in handy. Being prepared for difficult times is the best way to survive those times and reduce disruption in your life.

Every Pot's Got to Sit on Its Own Bottom

Unless you really like not knowing where your next meal is coming from, whether you'll have a place to live and clothes to wear, whether you'll have a way to get medical attention if you get sick or hurt; unless you want to live to get old and look back on your life and think about all the things you really wanted to do but couldn't, it's best to make sure you're able to take care of yourself.

Living your life with the expectation that someone will always be there to take care of you is like playing the lottery—a lot of people pay to play, but very few win. While there are many good people in the world, you can't always count on the same kind of "looking out for your neighbor" behavior that was more common when most people lived in small towns and rural communities. Today people often don't even know those who live on their block or in their apartment building. If they do, most times they don't have a strong enough connection to get help from them when a problem arises. Therefore, it is important to not only live your life for today, but also be prepared to take care of tomorrow. It is important to make sure you have the education, training, knowledge and skills to make it through life not only while you're young, but as you get older.

There is nothing wrong with wanting to have someone be there for you. There is nothing wrong with looking for and accepting help from someone when you need it. But if you don't have family, a *dependable* network of friends, or a program or organization that has your back, what is your plan B, C, D, E, F, etc. for making it through life with as little drama as possible? What is your plan for living the lifestyle you want to live if someone else isn't there to make it happen? What is your plan for having a comfortable old age where you *know* you will be able to pay for the care you need?

It's nice to think there will be someone there to help you with these things, but there might not be. Even if you have family or good friends, something beyond their control could prevent them from being there for you at the level of need you have. There's an old saying from down South: "Every pot's got to sit on its own bottom." What this means is the only way to make sure you have at least most of your bases covered, and your life has a good chance of turning out the way you want it to is for *you* to take care of *you*.

You can't know, predict or prepare for everything that might happen in life, but you can reduce the impact of surprises by not leaving everything to chance. Living life without a plan for dealing with your current and future needs is like jumping out of an airplane without a parachute—the free fall may be exciting, but the final landing will be very unpleasant.

BE SURE YOU HAVE
MULTIPLE SOURCES OF INCOME

When my parents were in their prime work years they could pretty much count on having a job for life and a pension to support them in their retirement years. Things were pretty much the same when I was in my prime work years. But today is totally different. Competition for jobs is global: you're not just competing with the people in your local area, but with people from around the world. You can do everything right and still find yourself unemployed. For the foreseeable future it's important to make sure you have more than one source of income.

A small part-time business is probably the most manageable because you'll have flexibility. To come up with ideas for a business, think about what you like to do or consider ways to turn a hobby into a business. The business does not have to be based on a product you sell. Service businesses offer some of the best opportunities. People today are very busy, and often feel overwhelmed by the demands of work, home and family. As a result, there are business opportunities for someone who can *reliably* assist with more routine activities. For example, some people have set up successful businesses that walk dogs, run errands, help people organize their homes or offices, or provide billing services to other small businesses.

If you decide to start a business, take advantage of training programs and services offered in most communities by the Small Business Administration, local colleges or universities or local non-profit organizations.

Running a business is not like being an employee. There are taxes, laws and other things you have to deal with when you own a business that you don't have to think about as an employee. One big difference between being an employee and owning a small business is: nothing happens unless you make it happen. For example, if you need paperclips you're the one that has to buy them.

If owning a business doesn't appeal, look for a part-time job that gives you the flexibility you need. Whether you start a business or take a part-time job, make sure you do something you like because this will make taking on extra work more tolerable.

Don't spend all the extra money you make. Open a brokerage account and invest as much as possible—50% or more if possible. This account can be used to build a strong financial foundation for things you may need or want: to purchase or put a down payment on a home, set up a flexible spending account to cover medical expenses, provide a cushion to cover emergencies, get an early start on retirement, develop a foundation or fund to support causes that are important to you.

Living comfortably throughout your life is possible, but it takes planning and preparation, and that involves making sure your total income isn't dependent on one job. There's an old saying: "Don't put all your (income) eggs in one basket." If your main job goes away and you have another source of income, you won't be totally broke immediately. You'll have some time and a financial cushion that allows you to make your next career move.

LEARN TO MANAGE AND INVEST YOUR MONEY

I found a notice in my pay check on my first job saying I would be eligible to buy stock in the newspaper where I worked through a payroll deduction plan after one year of employment. The notice said I could purchase stock for 13% less than the price a non-employee had to pay. Now math has never been my strength, but even I could figure out that I'd make a 13% profit the moment I bought the stock. I signed up for the stock purchase plan as soon as I was eligible.

Not knowing anything about the stock market, I walked over to the business editor and asked him to teach me about stocks, bonds and whatever else I needed to know to invest wisely. He gave me the basics and then gave me some ideas about books and articles to read to learn more. I followed up on his suggestions, and started reading the business pages. When I had periodic questions, he would answer them for me. I also opened up an investment account with a brokerage firm.

Although I was making less than $10,000 a year, living in a very expensive city, paying for a car as well as my other living expenses, and planning to get my teeth straightened, I still managed to take $25 out of each paycheck and put it in a savings account I had opened to hold the money I planned to invest. At the end of each year, I took my roughly $600 to the brokerage firm and bought solid stocks that had the potential to increase in value, *and* paid an annual dividend (something like interest). Instead of having the brokerage firm send me the dividend checks, I let that money accumulate, added it to what I could save from my paycheck and bought more stock in other industries. When I went to my next job, I signed up to have the maximum amount of money withdrawn from my check to invest in a company-sponsored retirement plan. The company matched part of what I took out of my check.

I continued to educate myself about investing and how to decide which investments to buy by reading books, magazines and newspapers, and by watching or listening to nightly business news programs on public radio and public television.

Over time I developed an investment philosophy which led me to:

- Establish a financial goal for myself—what kind of lifestyle I wanted in my retirement, and how much income it would take to achieve that lifestyle.
- Develop an understanding of my investment personality—my risk tolerance. I determined I'm a calculated risk taker. I'll take risks that make sense in terms of my financial goals, but I won't shoot craps (buy stocks based solely on a "hot" tip from a friend).
- Work with a reputable licensed and regulated brokerage firm.
- Partner with my broker. I didn't just do things because he or she said so. I asked questions until I understood why a recommendation made sense in terms of my long-term goals. I called to discuss investment ideas so I could understand why the idea did or did not make sense in terms of my long-term goals. If something happened in the economy (good or bad), I talked over what this meant in terms of any adjustments I needed to make in my investment portfolio. The closer I got to retirement age, the more conservative my investment approach became.
- Diversify my investments. Most people are scared to death and want to buy savings bonds or certificates of deposit (CDs) only. Your investments should include fixed income assets such as bonds, CDs, and Treasury notes and bills. But because these investments pay a fixed amount, the income they generate will not always keep up with inflation (the increase in what you have to pay for things you buy). If the cost of food, for example, increases faster than the amount of money a bond, CD, or other fixed investment pays, that's a problem. So, it's important to buy *quality* stocks in different companies *and* industries. Doing this will help ensure you don't get stuck with

one bad investment that totally wipes you out. And, it helps improve the likelihood that you'll generate enough money to pay your bills and live comfortably because good stocks generally grow in a way that keeps up with (and sometimes exceeds) inflation. Now, stocks don't go up in value all the time. But over the long term, they tend to grow in value. Since the goal of investing is to make money on *something* no matter what is happening in the economy, it's important to invest in both fixed assets (bonds, CDs, etc.) and stocks.

- Invest for income (interest, dividends) and growth (an increase in the dollar value of the stock). Pay attention to what's happening in the news and think about what opportunities that opens up for investment. For example, a story ran in the newspaper some years ago about Hong Kong (the center of Asian finance at the time) being taken over by mainland China, and financial institutions moving their money elsewhere. I asked my broker where the money was going. The answer: Singapore. I bought stock in Singapore Airlines. Today, anything "green" (environmentally friendly) looks like a growth investment area. But, check it out for yourself.

My goal had always been to retire around age 50. I was able to semi-retire at 55. At 59 1/2, I became eligible to take money from my investment account, which allowed me to retire completely if I wanted to. I work part-time because I want to, not because I have to.

I never made $60,000 a year on any job in my life. But because I learned about investing early and was disciplined about doing it, I'm able to live comfortably in my retirement years. Not only can I take care of my needs (food, clothing and shelter), but I can do things I enjoy doing. I have a season ticket to Milwaukee Bucks basketball games and Milwaukee Repertory Theatre plays, among other things.

Investing and preparing for retirement doesn't mean you can't do things for fun. When I was working full time, I didn't live like a hermit. I've bought a house, three cars (over the years), traveled, and done other things I like to do. I just made sure I not only lived for today, but planned for tomorrow.

You don't have to be wealthy to live comfortably throughout your life. But you do have to make a commitment to learn to manage and invest your money, and be disciplined about leaving that money alone until you retire.

Investing properly is a good way to make your money make additional money, even when you're asleep. So, before you invest keep these guidelines in mind:

- **Define what your investment goals are**: are you saving money for your education, trying to build a rainy day fund so you have money in case of an emergency or other unexpected event in your life, putting away money for retirement or all of the above?

- **Understand what your risk tolerance is.** Some people can take big chances without losing sleep over it, others can't. Some risk is inevitable when you invest. The question is how large a risk can you tolerate? As I said, I am a moderate risk taker. I invest so that, whatever happens, there's little chance I'll be wiped out completely. That's why I invest for income and growth—so that I have more than one way to make money. This paid off during the 2008 economic collapse. While I lost some money on paper, I didn't have to go back to work full time. And, my investments are making a comeback.

- **Read books and news articles on the subject.** Also, listen to or watch business news shows to understand what is going on in the economy.

- **Find a reputable firm**—one with a proven tract record of earning its clients money—to handle your account. Based on stories about people losing their life savings while investing with private investors, I suggest using established publicly traded firms that are regulated by the government. But no matter how good the firm is, don't just do what someone tells you to do. Do your homework so you understand how stocks, bonds, Treasury Notes and other investments work. *Before you agree to buy an investment, ask questions until you understand what's entailed and how the recommendation helps you achieve your financial goals and objectives.*

- **Keep an eye on what's going on with your account.** If something doesn't look right or you have a question or concern, contact your financial advisor. Don't wait for them to contact you.

- **If your investments are *consistently* not moving you toward your financial goal, don't hesitant to change financial advisors.** No investments are 100% perfect. There will be ups and downs. But, if you're *consistently* noticing problems in achieving your financial objective, it may be time to change brokerage firms.

Following these guidelines and living *below* your means (spending less than you earn) will all but guarantee you'll have a financial future that is better than average.

Do Look Back — for the
Right Reasons

Normally I don't believe in looking back or thinking about the past. But, there are advantages to doing this periodically:

- To see where I've come from. If you have set ambitious goals for yourself, you could be so focused on the fact that you're not there yet that you forget how far you have come. Looking back to see the distance you have traveled from your starting point will help encourage you.
- To make sure I'm on track with the goals I've set for myself. Given the fast-paced existence most of us live, it's easy to forget where you are in your life's journey, and it's easy to get sidetracked. By looking at where you are compared to where you said you want to be, you can get and keep your life moving in the right direction.

There is also a reason *not* to look back: to beat yourself up for something you did or didn't do. The bottom line is that no one makes a climb straight up to their dreams. Everyone moves in fits and starts, making progress and then losing ground. Those who get where they want to be in life are the ones who learn from their mistakes, make changes, and are persistent in their efforts. Throughout human history, the most successful people have not been those who did things perfectly all the time, but rather those who kept going despite setbacks. They learn from their mistakes, make changes (as necessary) to what they're doing, and keep pushing toward their dreams. This is true of those in every field: human rights, business, the arts, education, politics, science and technology, sports, you name it.

So look back on your life every now and then for the right reasons—to see where you've come from and determine whether you're traveling the road that will take you *toward* your dream. If the answer is "yes," celebrate!

KEEP YOUR OPTIONS OPEN

You never know what opportunities life may present you. That's why it is important to keep your options open so you can take advantage of the unexpected.

My junior year in high school I decided to become a newspaper reporter. Being a writer and doing something that would help others have always been my long-term goals. Journalism offered me the opportunity to do both. After graduating from Syracuse University and getting my master's degree from the University of Wisconsin—Milwaukee, I went to work for the *Miami Herald*, one of the top 10 newspapers in the country. I had worked there five years before I decided to look for other job opportunities. Miller Brewing Company, which at the time was a subsidiary of Phillip Morris—a *Fortune* (magazine) 500 company—had a representative at a job fair on Miami Beach. They were looking to hire a speech writer for the executives. It had never crossed my mind to leave the field of journalism. But it seemed I would not get a chance to become an editor at the *Herald* (which I wanted to do). I decided to take the job at Miller because I thought the opportunities for growth and development of new skills were greater there. My thinking was that, with new skills, I could get back into journalism at a higher level some time in the future.

The move to Miller opened up an array of options that had never crossed my mind. After writing speeches for a while, I began to do general public relations work, which required me to interact with just about every department in the company. Doing this helped me see first hand how a well-run company functions. I became a manager, which required me to develop a written plan for marketing the brands I was responsible for. The plan had to contain ideas for events, sponsorships, and news stories that appealed to the primary consumer of those products. It also had to include the steps needed to carry out the plan, a list of who was responsible for each step, and a list of expected results and benefits the plan would create that helped Miller's financial bottom line. I had to create a budget for carrying out my plan, and account for every dollar spent. The job also required me to hire and manage outside contractors that worked on projects with me, and provided me with an opportunity to hire businesses owned by people of color and women (many of whom were getting opportunities to do work for Miller for the first time). As part of the hiring process, I had to evaluate and (in a few instances) mentor the first-time firms. As a manager, I also had opportunities to attend workshops and seminars that sharpened my business skills. Working as a manager gave me a virtual master's degree in business administration.

While working at Miller I learned that the local public television station was looking for freelance producers for a new show—*Milwaukee Profiles*. It not only sounded interesting, but I also saw the opportunity as a way to acquire another set of new skills related to broadcast journalism. I used my newspaper background and my knowledge of the community to land one of those part-time jobs. I focused on doing positive stories about people in Milwaukee's African American community. This experience taught me how to edit video and write scripts for television news and features.

Later I used my journalism skills to teach news writing at the Milwaukee Area Technical College (MATC), which gave me teaching credentials.

After working for 10 years at Miller, I started my own business. For years, my business focused on helping companies market their products and services. But, as the number of offers to do marketing research increased, I developed the skills to do that also. Later, I had the opportunity to purchase and publish a business directory, which helped me develop desktop publishing and graphic design skills.

The skills I picked up as a journalist, at Miller, while working for public television, teaching at MATC, and running my own business set me up to accept an offer to run a small business development program at the University of Wisconsin—Milwaukee (UWM). I stayed for 17 years, which made me eligible to receive a pension and semi-retire at 55. A few years later my marketing skills, business/

business development skills, and network of relationships with a wide range of people in the community (acquired through both work and volunteer activities) helped me land a job working in a Congressional District Office doing small business development outreach as well as outreach to Milwaukee's faith and African American communities.

None of these additional experiences would have happened had I not been willing to keep my options open. Instead of sticking to my original plan—to be a journalist all my life—I looked at each new opportunity as a chance to learn, grow, and (in a variety of ways) do something to help others.

So, when a new opportunity comes along, look at it seriously. Don't automatically dismiss doing something because it's new or challenging. Instead, think about how the opportunity relates to those things you value most in life, and what new career, personal growth and community service paths this opportunity could lead to. Don't be afraid to shift gears. Doing so could not only move your life in interesting, productive and satisfying directions, but also give you a chance to make a positive difference in the world in ways you could not have imagined.

TAKE CALCULATED RISKS

If you want to get the most out of life, you have to take some risks. The only way to be completely "safe" is to do nothing. But often the "reward" for doing nothing is a life that gives you little reason to get out of bed in the morning.

The people we remember most in life are not those who say "That's the way it is because that's the way it's always been." Rather, those we remember are people who are willing to move out of their comfort zone toward their vision.

I believe in taking risks, meaning I'm willing to try new things. All risk taking is not the same, however. There is fly-by-the-seat-of-your-pants risk taking and calculated risk taking. Fly-by-the-seat-of-your-pants risk taking involves doing what comes into your mind without thinking about what might happen as a consequence of your actions. Calculated risk taking involves trying something new or different *after* you think about what could go right *and* what could go wrong. The first type of risk taking is a crap shoot—rolling the dice. You don't have any control over the outcome. You may learn what *not* to do if you take this approach to risk, but you will learn the hard way, which isn't fun. Also, you run the very real risk of your actions having disastrous long-term affects. The second type of risk—calculated risks—reduces your chances of doing something that could produce disastrous results that negatively impact you for the rest of your life.

I believe in taking calculated risks. When deciding whether to pursue a new opportunity, I follow two hard and fast rules:

- I won't do anything that will hurt me.
- I won't intentionally do anything that could hurt others. I include this second rule because my goal is not just to "do my thing." The universe doesn't revolve around me. Because I have been blessed with life, I have a duty to make the world a better place. As Shirley Chisholm, the first African American woman elected to Congress said, "Service to others is the rent you pay for your room here on earth."

When faced with a choice about whether or not to try something, I follow a process. I think about:

- What could happen to me in the short term if I do what I'm thinking about doing—what could go right and, more importantly, what could go wrong.
- What impact my actions could have on achieving my dreams and goals—will they help or hurt my chances?
- Whether I'd want to see a story about what I did on the front page of the newspaper or as the lead story on the evening television news. I don't want to do anything that would embarrass my family or me.
- Whether what I'm thinking about fits into my value system—what I consider important in life.
- Whether what I'm thinking about doing fits into what I hope will be my legacy—what I will be remembered for.

This sounds like a lot, but it really doesn't take forever. Sometimes I can get through my checklist in a few minutes. Other times I may sleep on it for a few days. If it's something that's potentially life-altering, I get really analytical: I write down the pros and cons of doing what I'm thinking about, and I pray for direction. After all this, I usually get a "feeling" about what I should or should not do.

If I go with that feeling, I usually end up making the right decision. Even so, I keep my eyes, ears and mind open for signs that I might need to reconsider the decision. The most obvious sign I'm moving in the wrong direction is that I keep running into barriers that prevent me from doing what I want to do. I don't give up right away. But, If I'm still hitting walls months later, I take a hard look at what I'm doing.

While the process of evaluating risks takes a little more time than doing the first thing that comes to your mind, taking that extra time makes it more likely you'll choose opportunities that allow you to learn something new *and* positive. Such learning helps you grow, become more well-rounded, and keeps life interesting for you personally and professionally. It also expands your understanding of the world, broadens your view of life, and increases the options life offers you. For example, my willingness:

- To travel to other parts of the country and the world has given me an opportunity to learn about and appreciate the differences *and* similarities we as human beings have, and to feel comfortable interacting in unfamiliar environments.
- To ask questions and learn about investing from a co-worker on my first job, which helped me retire early.
- To take on new assignments (both on the job and as a volunteer), which helped me develop skills and establish relationships with a wide range of people I might not otherwise have come to know.

Because I've been willing to take calculated risks, I've been able to live an interesting and enjoyable life that makes getting up in the morning fun because of all the opportunities each new day brings.

ALWAYS GIVE YOUR BEST EFFORT

Everything you do is a reflection of who you are as a person. That is why it is important to remember there is no such thing as a small or unimportant task. When you do the small things well, people trust you to do bigger and bigger things. As you do these bigger and bigger things well, you *earn* a reputation for being the "go to" person for getting things done right, on time and within budget. Having this reputation can bring additional opportunities, recognition and long-term success.

I used the word "earn" intentionally. You don't get to be president of a company, for example, without first demonstrating that you know how to do your job well at a lower level. There are *some* people who can fake their way to the top, but they usually don't have staying power. More often than not, they crash and burn because their success is not built on a solid foundation of skills, knowledge and discipline that can keep things functioning at a high level over the long term. They reach a point where they aren't competent to do their job, and mistakes happen. Their whole world comes apart the way a knit sweater can when you pull on a hanging thread.

In addition to giving your best effort because it is good for your reputation and your long-term career success, giving your best effort is also important because it is good for your long-term success in life overall. You get out of life what you put into it. If you give your best effort, you will get your best results. Part of the reason for this is that every situation you find yourself in teaches lessons you can use as you move through life. These lessons might be how to work more effectively with others, how to work through a problem and find a solution, or what *not* to do. All of these lessons can help you reduce the amount of drama in your life.

When you give your best effort (which requires you to pay attention to what you are doing, determine what other resources and support you need to do your best, and identify who best can help you) you will always learn something new. You will also sharpen your skills, which will help you face future challenges with more confidence.

So always do your best, no matter how small the task may seem at the time. It will pay off in the long run.

The Art of War

I have an "enemies" list: a list I have been keeping since childhood. The names on that list are people who have tried to harm me in some way—people who, I tell myself, will want to "act like they know me" as I achieve success in life. This may sound silly or egotistical, but it's how I have dealt with problem people all of my life. This technique has also helped me keep my eyes on the prize—what I'm trying to achieve—and kept me focused on being the best I can be. Instead of thinking about how I can get back at someone, I think about what I need to do to achieve my goals, get around the roadblocks and obstacles people throw in my path, and make a difference in the world.

I believe those who mess with me are trying to keep me from succeeding. They want to distract me, get me to focus on the negative (like getting back at them) rather than the positive (like living a productive life). The best way to "get back" at them is to do what they don't want me to do—succeed.

How do you keep focused on the positive? This may sound strange, but learning the game of chess gave me skills to deal with those on my enemies list in a way that does not derail my life and my dreams. Let me explain. To even have a *chance* to win in chess you not only have to think about the moves you're going to make, but you have to think about the moves your opponent *might* make. Then you have to decide how to counteract your opponent's moves in a way that places you in the best position to both avoid harm *and* win the game. What does this have to do with life? Achieving success involves:

- Planning how you're going to get where you want to go.
- Counteracting the efforts of those who try to stop you from getting there.

Many people don't think far ahead. They just react to the moment. When you react like this, it puts the other person in charge of the situation. Personally, I don't want anyone pulling my strings like that.

Going to "war" with my brain rather than my fists has, over the years, given me the satisfaction of seeing the dumbfounded look on the faces of those who can't figure out how I succeeded despite their best efforts to prevent that success. On several occasions I've had the opportunity to watch them squirm when, years later, the tables have turned and I'm in a position to decide whether or not they get to do something they really want to do. In those cases, I don't try to get back at them. Instead, I look at the situation as objectively as I can and make my decision based on whether they're the best person for the job or opportunity. In some cases the answer has been yes, in other cases no. Either way, having made a decision in as fair a manner as possible, my conscience is clear.

Having watched them squirm, I mentally check people off my "enemies" list—my list of those who want to "act like they know me"—and move on with life.

Always Have a Mountaintop You Want to Reach

One of the things that makes you want to get up in the morning is having goals that keep life interesting for you. I call it always having a mountaintop you want to reach—something you find challenging, something you want to achieve. At different points in your life that mountaintop may be different. When you're in school the mountaintop may be:

- Doing well in a subject that is hard for you.
- Participating in a school activity that you enjoy but may not be really good at, or that forces you to move outside of your comfort zone.
- Getting the knowledge and credits you need to get into college, trade school and the career you want.
- Getting experience by working or volunteering in the field you want to work in so you can confirm it's what you want to do. If so, the next step is earning credentials that demonstrate to a future employer you can do the job well.

Once you start working the mountaintop may be:

- Advancing in your career.
- Starting your own business.
- Establishing your own household.

- Creating the lifestyle you want.
- Preparing for life after work (both financially and in terms of how you want to spend your time).

As you get older—even before you reach retirement age—your mountaintop may change from things to something less concrete. If you have prepared yourself well for your career, worked hard, and managed your money well, you may find you have accumulated a lot of "stuff," and that getting more "stuff" no longer appeals to you. At this point you start to realize that what matters more to you are the people in your life: family, friends, those you can help reach their life goals, those that you know have your back. You also start thinking about what your life means in terms of its lasting impact.

While there certainly is nothing inherently wrong with "things," they will never give you the full sense of satisfaction that relationships and making a difference in the lives of others can. Building and maintaining close relationships, and reaching out to help others are achievements that will be there for your lifetime and beyond.

Whatever phase of life you're in—whether it's getting the knowledge and skills you need to achieve your dream, working to achieve your dream or building the type of legacy you would be proud of—always have something to strive for (a goal) that gives you a good reason to get out of bed in the morning. It will help make living enjoyable and rewarding.

BABY STEPS CAN GET YOU
WHERE YOU WANT TO GO

Writing books, plays and other creative works is something I have always wanted to do for a living. But as I have told people over the years, I had habits I couldn't kick—food, clothing and shelter. So I used my writing talents in other ways that were not as risky as sitting in a room for months and producing something that might not provide income to support those habits:

- **I worked as a newspaper reporter**. It was a job I loved, and one that helped me sharpen my writing skills and reinforce the gift of curiosity my parents gave me. The work also allowed me to have a positive impact on people's lives by shining a spotlight on issues and situations that needed changing.

- **I worked in the marketing department of a major corporation**, where my writing talent was used to write speeches for executives and, later, to develop marketing materials to support the brands I was responsible for. In my last five years on that job I managed a budget, which gave me the opportunity to hire businesses that, in the past, had limited success doing business with the corporation.

- **I worked part-time as a freelance producer for the local public television station where I learned to write for and edit video.**

The job allowed me to present a different, more positive and broad-ranging view of Milwaukee's African American communities. I later used these production skills to develop videos for a business development program I ran at the local state university.

- **I taught creative writing, attended writing workshops, wrote a play that was performed in public school, and the libretto (lyrics) for an opera.** Twenty years later I met composer, arranger and musician Neal Tate, who wrote the music for the opera. These experiences allowed me to help others sharpen their writing skills and gifts, as well as share my writing talents with others.

- **I started my own business**, which allowed me to provide employment for others; gave me opportunities to expand my marketing skills to include marketing research, develop additional skills such as desktop publishing, and expand my contacts in and knowledge of the local business community.

- **I ran an award-winning small business development program in the University of Wisconsin-Milwaukee's School of Business for 17 years.** The skills obtained running my own business helped me better understand the forces that helped small businesses succeed and the forces that created barriers to their success. Armed with this understanding, I was able to help individuals start successful companies that provided employment—including in areas of the city with high unemployment. When the state government ordered budgets cut, I knew my program would likely be cut because it was a non-degree, non-credit course that could not be used to help the university meet its accreditation requirements. Since I was a few months shy of qualifying for early retirement, I negotiated an agreement that allowed me to stay employed until I reached retirement age—55.

- **Shortly after leaving the university I worked on a political campaign.** That led to a part-time job that allows me to use the contacts and business development skills accumulated over the years to help make a difference in the community by helping the elected official I work for serve her constituents.

In my spare time I've started writing books, plays and other creative works.

Sometimes I wonder whether I might have been further along in my creative writing career had I started focusing on that goal earlier. However, as I look back, I see where each step I took in my career was a baby step that enabled me to sharpen my writing skills, acquire other skills that help me bring my literary works to market, have a level of economic security that makes life less stressful, and (hopefully) will allow me to leave a legacy through my writing that makes a difference in someone's life.

You don't always have to take giant leaps to get where you want to in life. Baby steps can also get you there.

YEAH, BUT

I run into people all the time who complain about how things are going in their life. They may be unhappy with a relationship. They may be unhappy with their job. They may be unhappy with their financial situation. They may be unhappy because they're having a hard time achieving their dream, or have not yet achieved their dream.

When I hear somebody complaining about the way things are in their life, my natural tendency is to try to help them change their situation. I don't try to tell them *what* to do. I just try to provide them with information, ideas, and options that might be helpful to them. I tell them about organizations or individuals that might be able to assist them; information from an article, book or other source they might want to look at; and provide examples of how others (including me) have dealt with similar situations.

I can pretty much tell from their response to our conservation whether their situation has the potential to change for the better. If they ask questions, ask for additional information, jot down ideas, ask me to send them information, follow through on suggestions and take the initiative to look for other ways to move their life in their desired direction, there's a good chance they are serious about making a change in their situation. And, there's a good chance they'll make progress in achieving the changes they want. If I hear the words "yeah, but" repeatedly, I pretty much know that the next time I see them—whether it's a month later, three months later, six months later—they'll be complaining about the same thing and will have made little or no progress toward changing their situation.

"But" is a powerful word. It *gives you permission* to not change anything that's going on in your life. Given that permission you, more often than not, won't *try* to make changes. "But" keeps your mind so focused on the walls between you and what you want that you often can't see the door right in front of you that may lead to the opportunity you say you want. "But" makes it easy for you to get discouraged when things don't go smoothly, and easy to tell yourself "well, I knew it wasn't going to work out anyway." "But" holds you down so you can't soar toward your dreams.

If you really want things in your life to change, *eliminate* the "but."

HOW BADLY DO YOU WANT IT?

I fulfilled one of my life-long dreams when I attended the Summer Olympics in Atlanta in 1996. One of the things that appeals to me is the Olympic ideal: that every competitor will give his or her best effort and, by doing so, is a champion whether or not they win a medal. Excluding those involved in cheating scandals, all those participating in the Olympics represent the best athletes their countries have to offer in each field of competition.

One of my favorite competitions is track and field—especially the sprints. The time difference between the runner who receives the gold and silver and (sometimes) the bronze medal is often a fraction of a second in track and field races. The difference in where runners finish is often determined by who leans into the tape first. That lean, to me, is a metaphor for what it takes to successfully compete in life: you have to be willing to throw yourself forward with your last ounce of strength to try to reach your dream.

Whatever you want in life—success in school, a job in which you have room to grow and develop, a successful business, a successful marriage and family, the ability to make a difference in the lives of others, a comfortable retirement—the question comes down to this: how badly do you want it? How much time and effort are you willing to put into preparing yourself—getting the education, knowledge and training you need? How much time and effort are you willing to put into doing things to the best of your ability? How much *extra* time are you willing to put into continually upgrading your knowledge and skills so you can be even better at what you do? How much time and effort are you willing to put into creating a plan of action so you can stay on track *and* carry out that plan? How willing are you to keep trying when things are not going well, or when others are telling you you can't make it? How willing are you to share your success with others? How willing are you to reach back and prepare someone else to take your place so you can continue to make a difference after you move on, or are no longer able to do the work yourself?

There is no guarantee you will finish first in everything you do. But if you're willing to give your best effort—to lean into the tape with your last ounce of strength—you *will* be a champion in life.

How badly do you want it?

Success Comes When You Carry Out God's Mission for Your Life

I had the chance to talk with the great playwright August Wilson once at the National Black Theatre Festival in Winston-Salem, N.C. One of the questions I asked him was whether he taught writing. He said no, his focus was on completing his mission of writing 10 plays about African American life in the 20th century.

Much to my dismay and the dismay of many who love theatre and love his work, he died shortly after completing his 10th and final play. Fortunately for the world his work (like that of Shakespeare, Eugene O'Neill, Arthur Miller, and Lorraine Hansberry) will live on stage as a testament to his greatness. The powerful, positive, multi-faceted images of African Americans he portrays in his plays will be available for future generations to see.

After his death, I realized how enlightening his response was. He knew his purpose in life, and he was focused on achieving that purpose. Wilson's single-minded focus brought him great commercial success, earned him two Pulitzer Prizes, and prompted the renaming of a theater in New York City's Broadway theatre district in his honor. News outlets worldwide covered his death and his life's work over a multi-day period.

When you do what you are put here to do, you will be successful at it. The trick is to identify what it is you were put here to do. I believe we all know instinctively what that is—it is the thing we always come back to. Given a choice, there is something (or somethings) we prefer to do. That's God's way of telling us which way we should go.

Unfortunately, we too often push that message aside and let outside forces influence us to do something else. We may tell ourselves that we don't have the education or the money or the right contacts to do what we want to do. But when we're doing what we were put here on earth to do, whatever we need to complete our mission will become available when we need it.

Our mission may or may not turn out to be our day job. Our job may give us the money we need to take care of our food, clothing and shelter so we can spend time carrying out our mission.

How can you identify your life's mission? The key is to take time to be still and listen to the voice inside you that is trying to break through the noise of the day and speak to your heart. That means turning off the radio, television, iPod—anything that can distract you—and finding a quiet place to think.

For me it also involves recording my ideas so I can come back to them and refine them over time. I happen to be a list maker, so I write down things that come to mind. I put them in order of preference—what would I most like to do? I pray for guidance, and make time to do what I have been led to do. You might find it easier to use a digital recorder first, and then listen to it or transcribe what you've said and read it; or you might use software that types what you say on your computer.

Whatever your mission is, it will have a *positive* impact on your life and the lives of others. If you're thinking about doing things that harm you or others, that's not your *true* calling. That's a diversionary force speaking, trying to take you off your game. Don't take that detour. Stay on the right track. The outcome will be pleasant and rewarding.

SUCCESS BREEDS SUCCESS

We've probably heard someone say "He (she) has all the luck" about someone who seems to succeed at whatever they do. I used to think that was true. But as I've lived life, I've come to realize that success is not so much about "luck" as it is about building upon past successes.

Those past successes don't have to be big things. If you're in school, building on past successes could be making the commitment to work hard and improve your grades in a particular class, and achieving that goal. Doing this could raise your grade point average, which will improve the options you have for college or other training, as well as your chances of getting funding to pay for this additional education. It will also increase your knowledge and skills, which will help you compete in the job market.

On the personal side, building on success could be deciding to lose weight, reduce debt by decreasing your spending, learning to control your temper, or finding the courage to try something new or difficult—and achieving those goals.

In the work environment, it could be getting training so you can move to another area of the company, to another job, or start your own business.

Each time you achieve a goal you have set for yourself you increase your ability to succeed because you develop a *track record* for doing what you set out to do. As a result:

- You increase your belief in yourself, because you can look back and see *proof* that you can do whatever you set your mind to do.
- You reduce your fear of trying something new because you've taken on new projects or activities in the past and completed them.
- People start to notice that you get things done and offer you other opportunities.

So, don't sell yourself short when you achieve "little" victories. Build on them. Step forward with greater confidence to tackle bigger and bigger goals.

And don't just rack up victories for yourself. Look for opportunities to make a difference in others' lives. Seeing how your actions help others will add to your confidence *and* satisfaction with your life.

MAKING A DIFFERENCE

Live Life on Purpose

We are busy people—always on the go. But even though we may do a lot of things, we don't always feel we've accomplished much at the end of the day. To feel accomplished, we need to live life on purpose—to set goals for ourselves and work to achieve those goals so we can see the progress we are making. I'm not talking about scheduling every moment and every activity in life. There needs to be room for spontaneity—time to take advantage of unexpected opportunities, down time to rest and give your mind a chance to think creatively, time to enjoy life. But as the saying goes, those who fail to plan, plan to fail.

I find it helpful to set five-year goals for myself—where I want to be and what I want to be doing five years from now. By setting goals and creating a plan for achieving these goals, I've been able to do many of the things I wanted to do. One of my goals was to retire when I was 50 years old. So, I started saving for retirement when I got my first job. I learned about investing, and worked with a broker to help me grow my retirement account safely while still being aggressive enough to generate income that would keep me living indoors in the winter and eating regularly throughout my "golden" years. I contributed the maximum amount of money to the retirement plans offered by the places where I worked, and became a serious bargain hunter. I seldom pay full price for major purchases, and I shop around to find the best price for whatever I need to buy. The result: I was able to semi-retire at age 55.

Having financial security has allowed me to do more of the things I want to do—including writing. Since people in my family generally live into their 80s and 90s (and a few 100s) I should, Lord willing, have many years of retirement ahead. In addition to eating and living indoors, I will be able to leave money for my nieces and nephew, and support a fund that donates money to causes that are important to me.

I decided to set up that fund because I wanted to make a difference long after my death. Since I don't have children, this would be a way to leave a legacy. I started by setting up an account separate from my personal banking account. Each year I put money—including all or part of my tax refund—into the account. When I mentioned the fund to my parents, they decided to contribute. We transferred the money from the savings account to an investment account. For special events like my 50th birthday, my parent's 50th wedding anniversary, my father's 70th birthday and his death, we asked that money be donated to our family fund rather than used to buy gifts or flowers. We're still growing the fund, but we have been able to provide small scholarships to students attending Historically Black Colleges and Universities.

All of my goals have not been "serious." When I got my first job, one of my goals was to travel and see other parts of the country and the world. I wasn't making enough money on that job to do a lot of traveling, but I found inexpensive trips to take on the weekend and during my vacation week. Over time I have been able to go to Senegal, West Africa and Brazil by connecting with the National Conference of Artists—a group of artists of Black African ancestry. The group was so large that the cost of travel was within my budget. I have also been able to go to Europe on a number of occasions: the first time with a former co-worker who had a brother in the military in Frankfurt, Germany. We used Frankfurt as our base of operation, and toured Europe using a Eurail pass—a train pass that allowed us to travel from one country to another while sleeping on the train for all but one night of our 10-day trip. Other times I was able to go skiing in Europe with members of my ski club and several other clubs that are part of the National Brotherhood of Skiers. Again, the group rates helped keep costs low.

Eventually (as my career advanced and I earned more income), I bought a time-share that allows me to trade my "week" at a resort where my time-share is located for a week in another location. That has helped me significantly reduce housing costs for vacations. I also signed up for airline frequent flier programs so I could accumulate enough miles to, eventually, get a free ticket.

I have been blessed to pretty much live the life I had hoped to live. I believe setting goals, planning, and executing the plan played a key role in turning my dreams into reality.

LET YOUR LIGHT SHINE

We're all put here for a purpose. God has given each of us one or more talents and a mission to fulfill within our lifetimes. That mission is part of God's plan to make the world a more perfect place. We were specially chosen before we were born to fulfill that mission. It is, therefore, our duty to use the talent or talents God gave us not just for our own benefit, but also for the benefit of others. We must not hide our talents but, rather, we must sharpen them so we can do our best in carrying out God's mission for our lives.

You may not think developing and using your talent matters, but it does. Think of yourself as a light bulb in a large illuminated sign. If your bulb is out, the missing light is noticeable and spoils the beauty and message of the sign. Not fulfilling your mission is like being that burnt out bulb in God's grand scheme for human life.

Letting your light shine won't always be easy. While some people will try to help you, there are others (sometimes many others) who will actively work against you. They'll say things such as, "Why do you want to do that," or "That's stupid" or "Why are you trying to be something you're not," or "You know it's going to be hard to do that," or "It'll take a long time to do that," or "*They* won't let you do that" because you're female or because you're not part of the "right" crowd, or because you're Black or Hispanic or Asian or Native American or because you come from the "wrong side of the tracks." The goal of these naysayers is to keep you from doing what God sent you here to do.

Some of what they say may be true. Doing what God would have you do might be hard. It might take a long time to do. You might not be part of the "right" crowd, or you may come from the "wrong side of the tracks." But remember: God equipped you before you were born with everything you need to carry out His mission for your life. If you're doing what He wants you to do, you will succeed. So seek God's direction for your life through prayer, and don't be afraid to step out on His will.

How will you know you're working within His will? He will help you over the rough spots, and clear a path through enemy lines and over obstacles—not necessarily on your timeline, but on His. He will give you the stamina you need to finish the job. He will give you inner peace and confidence. He will put people in your life when you need them who will help you carry your mission forward.

I know from personal experience that, by carrying out God's will for your life, you will not only receive your reward in heaven but in this life, too. I have been blessed with good health. My mother is still alive. I have had opportunities to travel both in this country and overseas. I am financially secure (not rich, but able to pay my bills and have enough money left over to do many of the things I enjoy doing). I am still excited about life and look forward to getting up each day. I have been able to do things that make life better for others, which has given me a sense of satisfaction. If I had drawn up a blueprint for my life, there is very little I would change. To be able to say that at a time when (based on life expectancy) I have a good chance of living another forty years is a blessing.

While I'm here, I plan to do what I can to let my light shine—to ensure my bulb in God's illuminated sign called life is on and bright.

Do the same. Let your light shine.

THERE IS MORE THAN ONE WAY
TO STAGE A REVOLUTION

Usually when people hear the word revolution they think of confrontations and violent actions. That is not necessarily the case. Other words for revolution include *change, reform, improvement, innovation, creativity* and *modernization*.

I learned there was more than one way to stage a revolution while I was in college in the 1960s. African American students during that time (following in the tradition of the non-violent Civil Rights movement for justice and equality) laid the foundation for a revolutionary change to create a better, more inclusive campus environment. While there were very few Black African-ancestored students on campus at the time (about 100 out of 10,000, including students from the continent of Africa) we demonstrated, boycotted, and advocated for a more diverse faculty and for changes in the curriculum that recognized the contributions that people of Black African ancestry had made to the United States and the world.

Some involved in the revolution were more assertive, vocal frontline warriors. Others, like me, worked more behind the scenes. At first I thought I wanted to be on the frontline. But after confronting dogs at the basketball field house when we marched there in protest, I knew frontline activism wasn't something I was prepared to do. So I became part of the group that discussed and planned next moves, and helped develop positions, strategies and "demands."

When other students marched on campus, those of us who weren't on the front line stayed in our dorms so it would look like all the Black students were involved in the march. It worked. We persuaded the university to start an African American studies program. We established the Student Afro-American Society (SAS), pushed to have more faculty and staff of color, and reached agreement with the university on a number of other issues. Over the years, the environment for students of color, while not perfect, improved. One of the African American's hired by the university came up with the idea for a "Coming Back Together" event to get African American and Latino graduates to become more engaged with the university. Many of us, once we graduated, did not come back to campus for homecoming or any other event, and we did not contribute financially to the University. The first event was covered by the *New York Times* and *Newsweek* magazine because Syracuse University was the first non-black institution to host an all-year reunion specifically targeting African American and Latino students.

The event was an amazing experience. First of all, to see so many Black graduates—some of whom had been students back in the day when Black students could not stay on campus—and to see the talent and brain power in the room made me remark to one of my classmates, "We could run the country from this room without help from any other group." Secondly, during a reception at his house, the Chancellor at that time (Melvin Eggers) said in his welcoming remarks that he knew when we were students at Syracuse we might not have felt welcome, but he wanted to assure us that the university considered us part of the family. And then, he did an extraordinary thing—he apologized for any experiences we might have had that made us feel unwelcomed and unappreciated.

Before we left, some of those in attendance got together to decide exactly what we wanted this event to be. The outcome of that discussion was that we didn't want it to just be a party and a good time (although social activities would certainly be part of the gathering). What we wanted was to interact with current students on campus to encourage them to stay there and graduate, and give them a picture of what the future could hold for them if they did. As a result, each "Coming Back Together" includes workshops and other activities designed to link graduates and students.

A number of years later, when the matter of contributing to the university was under discussion, the alumni of color decided any contributions made to the university should specifically benefit students of color. The "Our Time Has Come" scholarship raised over $3 million from alumni, friends, foundations, and corporations.

We helped revolutionize (change and improve) Syracuse University without violence.

The Only Thing Necessary for Evil to Triumph is for Good People to Do Nothing

You hear and read so many negative things in the news that it would be easy to become discouraged and think there is nothing you can do to change things for the better. There are wars and rumors of wars, killings and other unspeakable acts by one human being against another, stories about failing schools, rising health care and uninsured families, recalls of products ranging from toys to medicine, and bad news about jobs and the economy.

Listening to this on-going litany of what's wrong can be overwhelming and make you feel hopeless. But I subscribe to the statement made by the ancient Roman philosopher Cicero who said, "Where there's life, there's hope." As long as you're inhaling air, things *can* get better. The key to making this happen is for *each* person to do what *they* can to make things better.

Human history is filled with people who have done that. Harriet Tubman, a slave, not only decided she wanted to be free, but that others should be free also. She risked her life repeatedly to return South and lead hundreds of enslaved people to freedom.

Rosa Parks decided it was time to change the rules about segregated seating on public buses, so she refused to give up her seat to a white man (as custom at that time required) and sparked the Montgomery bus boycott that lead to the modern civil rights movement.

Marva Collins decided she was tired of seeing Black children failing in school, so she started her own academy where she set high expectations for achievement and helped children from tough neighborhoods that others had given up on meet those expectations.

Even small acts by individuals can make a difference. There is a story that is sometimes used in sermons about a storm that washed thousands of sea shells up on a beach. A man walking along the beach saw a young boy picking up shells and throwing them back into the water. He watched the boy for a long time and realized he wasn't just idly throwing the shells in the water. He seemed to have a purpose in mind. So the man asked the boy why he was being so diligent about throwing the shells back in the water. The boy said if they didn't get back into the water, they would die. The man looked at all the sea shells on the beach and said, "Look at all these shells. There are too many of them. You're not going to make a difference." The boy picked up another shell and threw it back into the water, turned to the man and said "I made a difference for that one."

While none of us can save the whole world by ourselves, each of us can do something on a daily basis to make a difference in someone else's life. It might be listening to someone who is having a bad day and offering words of encouragement, or finding someone who can help them. It might be becoming a peer counselor in school to help calm down situations that are heating up *before* a fight breaks out. It might be making a pact with like-minded friends that you're going to encourage each other to do well in school, *and checking* someone when he or she starts to stray from their promise. It might be saying a kind word to a young child who only hears how bad they are. It might be taking time to talk to or visit an older person who doesn't have family so they know someone still cares about them, or offering to cut their grass or shovel their snow at no cost to help them out. It might be marching in a rally to end violence and promote peace.

There are any number of things we can do to make things better. All we have to do is look around and decide where we want to make a difference, and then take action.

I believe there are more good people in the world than bad, and that when good people stand together they can block the evil intentions of those who would inflict harm on others. I agree with something Irish political philosopher, politician and statesman Edmund Burke said: "The only thing necessary for evil (things that harm others) to triumph is for good people to do nothing."

If each of us commit to stand up and take action against evil, our communities and our world will be much better places in which to live.

YOU DON'T HAVE TO GIVE
BIRTH TO BE A MOTHER

Mothers are not just those who give birth. They are also those who provide the caring, guidance, support, and positive direction that can help a young person become a successful, caring, productive adult.

I never had children, but I have tried throughout my life to do what I can to help young people navigate through life. I have served as a mentor. I have spent time in schools sharing my life and career experiences, and talking about how I managed to get through tough times. I have served on boards of organizations that help young people and families.

I've learned over the years it's not about doing "big" things. Sometimes something as simple as taking time to listen to and talk with a younger person can make a difference. Sometimes taking time to play with a small child or say something complimentary about them can make a difference. Sometimes something as simple as a smile and a "Hi" can positively impact how that child's day goes.

I am also a firm believer in what I call the "teachable moment"—taking advantage of a situation a young person is experiencing at that moment to point out something that can help him or her make a decision that will help, not hurt, them in the future, or a decision that will make them feel more confident in their ability to become whatever they choose to be.

Sometimes having a positive impact isn't even about direct action. Children learn by observing what others do—especially adults. If they see adults dealing with situations by blowing up, fighting, lying, taking advantage of others—that's what they'll do because they think it's right. If they see adults talking out their problems in a calm manner, working together, helping others, being fair—that's what they'll do. I've had people I've known as children tell me they learned how to deal with different situations by watching what I did and how I carried myself. I never knew they were watching!

Being a mother is all about doing whatever you can to nurture a child and help him or her grow up to be a successful positive, productive, caring adult. In that sense, all females can be mothers.

MAKING A BABY AND BEING A FATHER ARE TWO DIFFERENT THINGS

Making a baby and being a father are two different things. Making a baby is about biology. Being a father is about being a parent—making sure the needs of the child are met even if it means giving up some of the things *you* want to do, and providing the caring, guidance, support and positive direction needed to help the child become a successful, caring, productive adult.

Parenting is not the function of one gender. My father played a significant role in developing me into the person I am today. I remember him taking time to attend my "tea parties" where we pretended to eat tea cakes made out of mud. I remember him teaching me to play and enjoy watching a wide range of sports. I remember him encouraging me to do my best academically and intellectually at a time when being smart and doing well academically was not considered a high priority for girls. I remember him buying me psychology books while I was in high school after I mentioned I might want to become a psychologist. He did this because he wanted me to get a head start on understanding the field. I remember him telling me I didn't have to take a back seat to anybody—that I could be anything I wanted to be. I remember him telling me how proud he was of me. Even during the later stages of his dementia when we were talking about nothing in particular, he would sometimes look at me, grab my hand, tell me to "go get 'em," and that he was proud of me. These things meant and mean a lot to me, and have helped me keep on pushing through whatever difficulties life presents. They also have inspired me to do what I can to help young people. I never had children, but I have tried throughout my life to do what I can to help young people navigate through life. I have served as a mentor. I have spent time in schools sharing my life and career experience, and talking about how I managed to get through tough times. I have served on boards of organizations that help young people and families, and donated money to organizations that help children.

Frequently, I've found, making a difference in a child's life is not about doing "big" things. Sometimes something as simple as taking time to listen to and talk with a younger person can make a difference. Sometimes taking time to play with a small child or say something complimentary about them can make a difference. Sometimes something as simple as a smile and a "Hi" can positively impact how that child's day goes.

I am also a firm believer in what I call a "teachable moment"—taking advantage of a situation a young person is experiencing at that moment to point out something that can help him or her make a decision that will help, not hurt, them in the future, or a decision that will make them feel more confident in their ability to become whatever they choose to be.

Sometimes having a positive impact isn't even about direct action. Children learn by observing what others do—especially adults. If they see adults dealing with situations by blowing up, fighting, lying, taking advantage of others—that's what they'll do because they think it's right. If they see adults talking out their problems in a calm manner, working together, helping others, being fair—that's what they'll do.

Children do not ask to come into this world. But once they're here, it's every adult's responsibility—males as well as females—to nurture (train, encourage, and support) that child.

Nurturing a child is what being a parent, a father, is all about. It is what will help that child grow up to be a successful, positive, productive, caring adult.

Money is a Tool, Not An End in Itself

Every where you look it seems the focus is on the *bling*. It's not good enough to have a pair of jeans. The jeans have to be a certain brand if you want to feel good about yourself. It's not good enough to have a television. It has to be a high definition, plasma or big screen television. It's not good enough to be able to listen to music, you have to have the *latest* electronic gadget to play your tunes.

Based on the images we see all around us, the goal in life is to get "more." There is no way to define what "more" means because new things are always being created and waved in front of our faces.

If you believe what marketers, advertisers, filmmakers, people in the television, music, and fashion industries are hyping, "more" means if you're not living the lifestyle of the rich and famous there's something wrong. Some people have acquired so much in the quest to get "more" they not only have a house or apartment (and maybe a garage) full of stuff, but they also rent storage space to hold the overflow.

Keeping up with the desire for "more," of course, takes money. But most of us don't and won't make "rich and famous" money. If we get a good education, work hard *and* smart, and manage our finances well, we will live comfortable lives. But "rich and famous" is not necessarily in our future.

Those who keep hyping "more" are diverting our attention from a very important fact—that money is a tool you can use to take care of yourself *and* to make a difference in the lives of others, but it is not a life goal. Money should not be the focus of your existence to the point where you love it and the things it can buy more than you love people and doing things for others.

Warren Buffett, a multi-billionaire and one of the riches men in the world, didn't set out to make big money. He found something he loved to do, and focused on doing it to the best of his ability. The money followed. He has used some of that money to establish the Buffett Foundation, and pledged most of the rest to the Bill and Melinda Gates Foundation—both of which support causes that benefit people in need. He has also auctioned off personal property and his time to raise money for other foundations and organizations that help people.

Don't get me wrong. When I say money should not be a goal, I'm not advocating living on bread and water and having only two outfits and one pair of shoes. There's nothing wrong with living comfortably. But, to paraphrase a verse from St. Luke in the New Testament, to whom much is given, much is required. The true value of money is not how much "more" it can buy, but rather how much of a difference it can make in the lives of those who are living closer to the margins of society. People like Oprah Winfrey, Bill Gates, Bill Cosby, Tom Joyner, Rachel Robinson (widow of Jackie Robinson, the first African American to play major league baseball), Bono, and Buffett have used the riches they have been blessed with to bless others.

None of us will be able to take all our stuff with us when we die. We need to use the money and other resources we have *temporary* possession of to help make the world a better place for those who follow us. By doing this we will leave something behind that lasts long after we are gone.

Leave a Legacy

What will people say about you at your funeral? That may sound like a morbid thing to talk about when you have your whole life ahead of you, but now is the time to begin building your legacy—your contribution to a better world.

If you think about it, everything you do on a day-to-day basis is part of that legacy. Do you:

- Treat people with respect even if you don't like them?
- Look for opportunities to help someone else?
- Act strictly based on what's in *your* best interest, or do you think about the impact your actions will have on other people?
- Encourage others or put them down?
- Support and cheer other people's success or try to undermine them?
- Stand up for what is right even if it is not the popular thing to do?
- Act to make positive change happen, or just talk about "the problem?"
- Do everything you can to develop your God-given talents so you can use them for your benefit *and* the benefit of others, or just drift through life?
- Take responsibility for your actions and learn from your mistakes, or blame everybody else when something goes wrong?

- Listen to others, learn from their experience and pass on this knowledge to others, or only focus on your ideas, opinions and what's happening to you?
- Create or participate in conflict or try to resolve it?

Your answers to these questions determine whether the legacy you leave can benefit others 100 years or more after your death.

We may not all end up in history books and become household names. But each of us, in our own way, is making history on a daily basis. Whether that history will be something to celebrate or something to forget depends on how we live.

Live to leave a legacy that others will celebrate.